ROCK & ROLL

...AND THE BEAT GOES ON

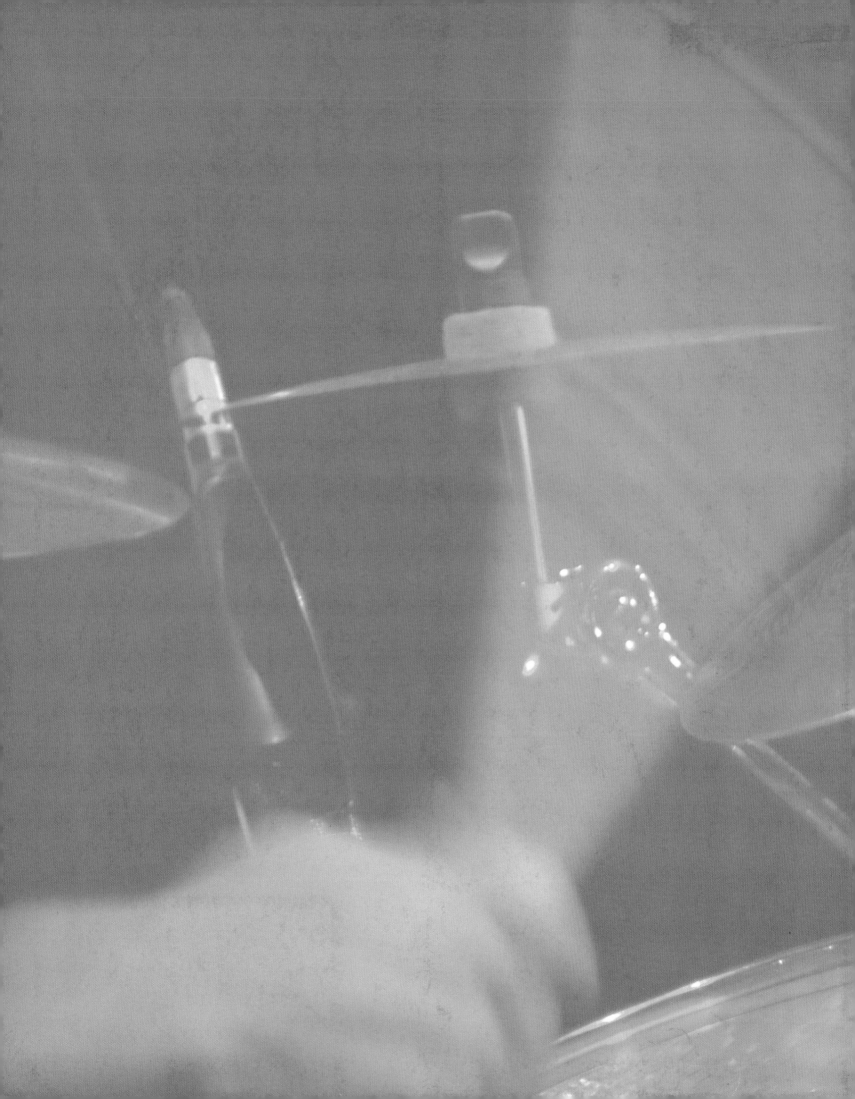

ROCK & ROLL

...AND THE BEAT GOES ON

"Cousin Brucie" Morrow

with Rich Maloof

Foreword by **Brian Wilson**

Preface by **Petula Clark**

Epilogue by **Billy Joel**

imagine!
New York
www.imaginebks.com

Library of Congress Control Number: 2009922017

1 2 3 4 5 6 7 8 9 10
Published by Imagine Publishing, Inc.
25 Whitman Road, Morganville, NJ 07751

First Edition.

Distributed in the United States of America by BookMasters Distribution Services, Inc.
30 Amberwood Parkway, Ashland, OH 44805

Distributed in Canada by BookMasters Distribution Services, Inc.
c/o Jacqueline Gross Associates, 165 Dufferin Street,
Toronto, Ontario, Canada M6K 3H6

Distributed in the United Kingdom by Publishers Group UK
8 The Arena, Mollison Avenue, Enfield, EN3 7NL, UK

Distributed in Australia by Capricorn Link (Australia) Pty. Ltd.
P.O. Box 704, Windsor, NSW 2756 Australia

Produced by BAND-F Ltd.
f-stop Fitzgerald, President

Karen Jones, Project Manager

Interior design and production by Maria Fernandez

Printed in China

ISBN-10: 0-9823064-3-1
ISBN-13: 978-0-9823064-3-7

For information about custom editions, special sales, and premium and corporate purchases,
please contact Imagine Publishing, Inc. at specialsales@imaginebks.com.

For my children Ion, Paige, and Meridith—who took the journey with me

and provided that special joy and love along the way

To my soulmate and my best friend, my wife Jodie, who played

a very important part in the writing of this book.

Jodie's insight and observations once again made for

an amazing partnership on this journey.

With Love,

Bruce

Table of
Contents

FOREWORD

by Brian Wilson

It should come as no surprise to readers when I say that a large part of my heart and soul belongs to music. My mother and father both played piano, and I remember my home being filled with all kinds of wonderful music. Growing up in California the 1950s, I idolized the multi-part harmonies of groups like the Four Freshmen. It didn't take long for my younger brothers Dennis and Carl and I to start practicing those smooth harmonies in our rooms.

I also had a strong feeling that if this style of multi-part harmonizing could be combined with certain rock rhythms, like those of Chuck Berry, there might be a new wave of music to experience. This was the early 1960s, and I wasn't the only one experimenting with new musical styles. Little did any of us know that everything about music was ready to change radically.

Our group went through several different names, including the Pendle-tones, but when my brother Dennis, who was a surfer, suggested we write about the new surfing craze, our path was set. We became the Beach Boys, singing about surfing, girls, hot rods, and "Fun, Fun, Fun" in the California sun with a string of songs that started with "Surfin'" and "Surfin' Safari." It was a wonderful experience then, and it is still very gratifying today to share the music that fills my heart and soul.

When I met Cousin Brucie at a radio station in New York City, it was obvious that he loves this music as much as I do. Our interview went so well that I knew I had found another "relative" in

"Cousin" Brucie. Years later, I still love listening to the sounds of the 1960s and I can think of no better music industry icon to bring this unique music, and the era, to life for readers than "Cousin Brucie" Morrow. He was there for the entire decade, introducing new artists to enthusiastic audiences and inspiring listeners to enjoy the "good vibrations." He is still doing so today.

—*Brian Wilson*

Brian Wilson is one of rock & roll's true icons. The long string of Top 40 hits he created with the Beach Boys, including "Surfin' Safari," "Good Vibrations," "California Girls," and "Help Me, Rhonda," launched an exciting and influential new sound for a new generation. His successful solo career includes the albums Imagination, Brian Wilson Presents SMiLE, *and* That Lucky Old Sun *among others. Brian Wilson is a member of the Rock & Roll Hall of Fame, the Songwriters Hall of Fame, and the UK Music Hall of Fame. He is a Grammy Award winner and is also a recipient of the prestigious Kennedy Center Honor, given for exemplary lifetime achievement in the performing arts.*

PREFACE

by Petula Clark

When I was growing up in the UK, I was mad about music, mostly swing. I loved the big bands and their great vocalists. Peggy Lee was my idol, along with Lena Horne and Patti Page. Of course, we had some very good singers in England, but we kids were dazzled by the sound of American jazz, blues, and eventually, rock & roll. Though this is what we strived to emulate, what was really happening was a curious cocktail of two musical cultures—the United Kingdom blending with the United States.

Finally, in the early 1960s, the Beatles arrived on the scene with a defining example of this potent mixture. The music was fresh, youthful, and sassy. Suddenly, the "British Sound" was born after years of bubbling under the surface.

The Beatles quickly opened the gates in the US for so many other talented UK artists, including some of us girls, such as the wonderful Dusty Springfield.

At the same time, music was changing throughout America. We were all listening to the New York–based folk of Bob Dylan and Peter, Paul & Mary, and the California sounds of the Beach Boys, the Byrds, and the Mamas & the Papas. There was also the amazing music of Detroit's Motown, with Smokey Robinson & the Miracles, the Supremes, and Marvin Gaye.

As for my involvement, "Downtown" was recorded in London at Pye Studios in October of 1964. Tony Hatch wrote, arranged, and produced this great song and many others for me such as "I Know a Place," "My Love," "A Sign of

I always felt that the disc jockeys who grabbed onto "Downtown" were very important to its success and helped make it a massive hit.

the Times," "I Couldn't Live Without Your Love," and "Don't Sleep in the Subway."

In December, 1964, "Downtown" was released in America by Warner Brothers Records. By January of 1965, it shot to number 1 on the American *Billboard* charts and I was soon to meet the American public for the first time via *The Ed Sullivan Show* on television.

I always felt that the disc jockeys who grabbed onto "Downtown" were very important to its success, and helped make it a massive hit. The song not only earned me a gold record and a Grammy, it launched my long and happy career in the US.

Meeting "Cousin Brucie" Morrow during his DJ days at WABC radio in New York was a big moment for me. I also recall he introduced some lively Coca-Cola jingles I recorded back then. I had heard so much about him and his enthusiastic style. But in the flesh he was, and still is, funny, knowledgeable, and a bit overwhelming! Seeing him again recently, while a guest on a PBS-TV special, was such fun. We laughed and talked about our shared experiences from those great years—and time stood still.

Thank you Brucie and keep at it!

Love,
Petula

Bobby Darin and Petula Clark on a 1967 Rodgers & Hart Today television special

One of the most successful female recording artists to hail from England, Petula Clark topped the American and international charts during the 1960s with million-seller "Downtown," earning her the first of two Grammy Awards. A string of hits followed, including "I Know a Place," "My Love," "A Sign of the Times," "This Is My Song," and "Don't Sleep in the Subway." Petula has performed concerts all over the world, in addition to starring in film and stage musicals as well as countless television appearances. An accomplished composer, Petula continues to make new recordings. Her latest albums are Open Your Heart, Duets, and Solitude & Sunshine.

INTRODUCTION

by "Cousin Brucie" Morrow

The Journey Continues

Cousins, feedback from our previous book, *Doo Wop: The Music, the Times, the Era*, has been amazing. We covered the early days of rock & roll through the prism of my personal experience, a bunch of beautiful photos, and a collection of memory-jarring reflections.

So here we are, ready to tackle the next era with new observations, fresh images, and a retelling of historical happenings that were sometimes so mind-blowing that in retrospect they seem fictional. The years and events covered in these pages were earth-shaking and head-shaking. Generations split, technology soared, and heroes rose and fell. The times were charged politically, racially, sexually, and socially, and probably represent the most dynamic years in our history.

I guess the pot had to boil rapidly before it was ready to blow steam—and, cousins, blow it did! Music, especially rock & roll, spread its wings and soared as an expression of the changing times. Radios and record players pumped out the message to an eagerly awaiting audience.

If you've ever looked closely at a record playing on a turntable—remember records and turntables? —you may have wondered how many hundreds or thousands of grooves are

THE WORLD WE'RE SPINNING ON WAS SHAKEN, WHICH CAUSED A LOT OF RACKET AND LEFT US PRETTY SCRATCHED UP. BUT AFTER THE NEEDLE JUMPS THE GROOVE, IT SETTLES BACK IN. AND THE BEAT GOES ON.

Cousin Brucie's personal
SIRIUS XM Radio bobblehead
"action" figure.

I've always thought of rock + roll as the soundtrack of our lives. The stylus comes down when you're born and rides along one continuous track. When it picks up at the center, well, let's hope you enjoyed what you heard!

carved into that black shellac. You can figure it out if you stare long enough: Cousins, there's just one. One long groove, from start to finish. Follow it along on a good rock & roll album, though, and you'll hear everything from thumping rhythms and dance beats to bittersweet ballads and soul-searching reveries. Every so often, there's a moment of silence.

I've always thought of rock & roll as the soundtrack of our lives. The stylus comes down when you're born and rides along one continuous track. When it picks up at the center, well, let's hope you enjoyed what you heard!

This book is just one man's take—just one groove, you might say—on the most remarkable and revolutionary era of the past century. It's not a musical encyclopedia or a complete cultural history. Rather, it's a document of the times I've had the good fortune to experience from the catbird seat of a radio studio. I've heard the voices of the people on phone lines and sent records of their emotional experiences back across the airwaves in the form of music.

It was a time of such dramatic change. Sometimes it all went smoothly, the music played, and everyone was happy. Other times, the world we're spinning on was shaken, which caused a lot of racket and left us pretty scratched up.

But after the needle jumps the groove, it settles back in…and the beat goes on.

—"Cousin Brucie" Morrow

CHAPTER I

The long and winding road to rock & roll

Mary Had a Little Lamb

Looking back now, it makes a lot of sense that the first recorded sounds were inspired by a song.

One very special moment more than a century ago, in 1877, sings out from the silent pages of history. That's the year Thomas Edison had the idea to wrap some tinfoil around a cylinder and etch sound vibrations into the foil with a needle. He figured that if another needle was run back through the same indentations, the sound would be reproduced.

Well, cousin Tom was right. He recited the nursery rhyme "Mary Had a Little Lamb" into the machine—and then the most incredible thing happened. He heard his own voice being played back. To Edison it was like holding up a mirror. Though his invention did exactly what he'd hoped it would, Edison said he was never so taken aback in his whole life. "Everybody was astonished," he's been quoted as saying. "I was always afraid of things that worked the first time."

Now hold on to your headphones, my cousins, because it turns out that Edison was not the very first person to record sound. Surprised? Well, you're not alone. In 1860—seventeen years before Tom and his tinfoil—a Frenchman named Édouard-Léon Scott

The earliest inventors of recorded sound could have chosen anything to record—a slamming door, children laughing—but they chose music.

de Martinville had used something he called the "phonautograph" to inscribe sound vibrations onto a piece of paper that had been darkened with smoke. Scott didn't have any way to play the vibrations back yet—unlike Edison, he hadn't dreamed that sound could be regenerated—but in 2008 audio experts from the Lawrence Berkeley National Laboratory in Berkeley, California, figured out a way to turn his paper scratches into sound using a computer. To their amazement, a female voice emerged from the paper—and from history—singing a line from the French folk song "Au Claire de la Lune." Through the distortion, the Berkeley scientists could hear her sing a line from the middle of the song as if they were glimpsing an everyday moment from a life lived long ago:

Under the moonlight,
Pierrot responded…

Can you imagine what it felt like to hear that 148-year-old voice playing back through a computer? Incredible.

There still seems to be a little magic at work when the needle hits the groove.

It's striking to me that both inventors turned first to music. Edison, it turns out, had a five-year-old daughter and two-year-old son at the time, so nursery rhymes must have been fresh in his mind. He and Scott could have recorded anything: their own names, a slamming door, children laughing…it could have been a shopping list. But they chose music.

Edison may not have been the world's first record producer, but he did figure out how to record *and* play back sound. Thanks to him, the phonograph was born. It was at that "Mary Had a Little Lamb" moment that technology and expression—the expression of the human voice—together sparked a change that would truly alter the course of our culture.

Today, we take recorded sound for granted. It's part of our lives. Just about every household in America plays back voices on answering machines and cellphones. You can record a list or a lecture onto a recorder the size of a wafer, and you can create music with a laptop computer. We enjoy our favorite tunes on CDs and MP3 players or zapped to us directly from a satellite. A few of us nostalgic types even continue to spin vinyl discs on phonographs—and there still seems to be a little magic at work when the needle hits the groove.

It seems kind of funny now, but when Edison came up with the phonograph, he was actually trying to invent a way to record telephone calls and telegraph messages. Far more than experimenting with cylinders and needles, Edison was interested in communication. Putting one human being in touch with another—that's what rock & roll is all about. More than shaking your booty, celebrating your life, or aggravating your parents, rock & roll is about communication.

So now you can start to see how Edison's phonograph put three big pieces of the rock & roll puzzle into place: technology, expression, and communication. And this was a good seventy-five years before anyone sang *Womp-bomma loobop, a-womp bam boom!* Boy, if only Edison had said that.

The phonograph's brilliant stroke was not just that it provided entertainment but that it provided entertainment *at home*. There's even an old advertisement of Edison standing over his invention accompanied by the words, *I want to see a Phonograph in every American household*. Well, sure he did—he was making twenty percent on every sale! But time would prove that what Edison envisioned was right in tune with what the public wanted. For the first time in history, there was the potential to listen to music in your own front parlor without having to survive Aunt Emma crooning her personal favorites.

It took a few years for Edison's invention to be refined for the general public. It had to become affordable, first of all, and those clunky cylinders would need to be flattened out into platters. By the 1910s, phonograph cylinders were indeed giving way to gramophone records, and people were starting to enjoy the freedom of playing thick, two-sided discs within their own four walls.

Remember that for years, even centuries, beforehand, the only way you could hear music was to go see live performances. Unless they were rich enough to sponsor a private performance, listeners didn't decide which songs were played— that was up to band directors and conductors. But now the turntables were turning, and people were starting to exert their own will on what they listened to. You might say it was really the first time that customers customized.

Jumpin' Jukes

If any one thing represented this huge shift toward personalized entertainment, it was the jukebox. Invented in 1915 and making the scene in the late 1920s, the jukebox was a spectacle of sight and sound. There had been coin-operated gramophones and player pianos before, but neither one rivaled the juke. You'd go into a bar—or in those days, a saloon—and standing in the corner would be this fantastic fixture ready to play your 78 rpm record on request.

THE ARC ON A JUKEBOX MADE IT LOOK LIKE A STAGE. PLAYING A FAVORITE SONG ON A JUKEBOX WAS LIKE A PRIVATE PERFORMANCE.

What big and beautiful boxes those original jukeboxes were. The first ones were made of oak and glass, and it wasn't long before the designs became more creative and elaborate. They would incorporate lights and chrome, all held together with a smooth and colorful plastic called Bakelite.

Through a domed window in the front you could see Edison's invention hard at work as records were retrieved and played under a mechanical arm. Some jukebox faces were even lined with narrow water tubes: the heated water would start to gurgle and send cool little strings of bubbles over an arc of incandescent lights. The arc made the

Putting one human being in touch with another—that's what rock + roll is all about.

face of the jukebox look like a stage: Playing a favorite song on a jukebox was like a private performance.

Rock & roll was still a good quarter century in the future, but it was already stirring inside those early jukeboxes. Entertainment, liberation, commercialization, personal expression, spectacle…this strange little set of qualities that characterized the jukebox experience would be matched one-for-one by the hallmarks of rock & roll.

The world wasn't ready quite yet. Mary's little lamb, all white and fluffy, was still the picture of purity.

Shaking the Blues

The word "juke" comes from an old Creole term meaning to get rowdy or unruly, and that was something of a prescription for the era of the late 1920s and '30s. It was a good time for jukebox joints and jumpin' jive. Why? Because the Great Depression was upon us, and everyone needed an escape. That's one of the amazing things about the human spirit: When times get rough, we can still turn adversity into celebration. Psychologists have noted that in uncertain economic times, listeners tend to prefer thoughtful songs—but that an upbeat rhythm can do them a world of good. People were waiting in bread lines and worrying where their next meal would come from, but they could still find a reason to dance. They wanted to shake off all of the hardships and darkness and remind themselves that the sun was going to come back out someday.

Because it was an age of great difficulty, not every selection on a jukebox made you get up and do the Lindy. The need for a pensive, soul-searching musical escape was served when the mournful sound of the blues came crying through those big boxes. Stripped of money and possessions, with old shoes worn through to the dirt, more people than ever began to identify with the pain and suffering they heard in the blues music created by African Americans. Strong rhythms, heartfelt melodies, and sometimes salty lyrics offered a gritty reflection of the times.

One particular song with all of these qualities can be traced back to the post–World War I years and a blues singer named Trixie Smith. In 1922, Trixie belted out a song called "My Man Rocks Me (With One Steady Roll)." When she sang the suggestive line of the song's title in a knowing voice, it marked the first time the phrase "rock & roll" was pieced together. If anyone questions whether rock has its roots in the blues, well, they'll have to answer to Trixie.

While Trixie was singing about what went on behind closed doors, the world outside was still reeling from World War I. All of the nation's hope and optimism, which had built so beautifully at the turn

of the nineteenth century, went up in ashes when we crossed the Atlantic to fight the Great War. America under Woodrow Wilson had tried to remain isolationist and cut off from the mayhem in Europe, but the world came calling. Our boys were going overseas.

Progress of every kind needs some kind of stimulus and, for better or for worse, the war was instrumental in pushing forward all kinds of technology we'd come to enjoy later in peacetime. One use of the phonograph that even Edison hadn't imagined was that soldiers could take music along with them overseas. Songs of patriotism, songs of freedom, songs about girlfriends waiting back home under the apple tree—they could all be packed up and played back by the homesick hero. (Ever the entrepreneur, Edison had his company develop a special Army-issue phonograph in 1917.)

Radio Days

Pre-recorded music may have helped establish an emotional link from shore to shore, but the phonograph wasn't going to be of much help strategically. When two-way communications became of paramount importance to the military, the greatest potential rested with the radio.

Wireless radio had been around for decades prior to the war, but it hadn't yet been mastered. Amateur technicians in the early 1900s had been tinkering with transmitters and trying to broadcast stronger signals over longer distances. A few wireless companies had even been established around the technology (the biggest being the Marconi Wireless Company, founded by one of radio's inventors, Guglielmo Marconi). But all of that came to an abrupt stop when the US entered the war, because the government made it illegal to operate transmitters and receivers. Like so many

aspects of American industry, all of the productivity and expertise had to be directed toward the war effort. Plus, the government didn't want to risk having sensitive information intercepted by the enemy.

Once the war ended and radio restrictions were lifted, news of the world around us came crackling over the airwaves. The difference was astonishing, like a curtain that had been blocking our view of the world was thrown back. Before the war, any news the public received came days afterward in the newspaper or came ticking over a telegraph word by word. But soon, with wireless technology greatly advanced and radios in every living room, happenings around the globe were relayed to the public instantaneously. Every listener's reach was as wide as the ocean.

Hearing those early broadcasts must have been something like Edison's eureka moment, when he heard his own voice on the phonograph. Only now the playback wasn't a simple nursery rhyme. Voices on the

With wireless radio, every listener's reach was as wide as the ocean.

radio relayed the savagery of war, the shifting lines on the map, the efforts to rebuild devastated cities. We were as fascinated to hear those voices coming through the speaker as we were repelled by what they sometimes said. Grateful for our safe havens and the homecoming of our sons, we knew now that the world was not such a safe place. Neither was it very far away.

The Never-Ending Dance

When a society starts looking around and sees what goes on outside its immediate neighborhood, as we did in the wake of World War I, things start happening. People start asking questions. When people start asking questions,

answers have to be ready. Time and time again, music provides those answers.

Music reflects every aspect of the era that creates it. The victories and losses, the celebrations and sorrows—they are all there in song as they are in life. As we'll see throughout these pages, music and culture depend on one another for creation and survival. The two spin around and around together, locked in a dance as old as the world.

The seeds of the rock & roll tree were planted, stamped down, and fertilized in the first half of the twentieth century. It was a troubling time, and we felt more than our fair share of growing pains. Some say we lost our way when we went to war—others say it was times like those that made us stronger individuals and strengthened the bonds with our brothers and sisters around the world. One thing for sure, though, is that those kinds of experiences come at the cost of innocence. The world wasn't flat or simple or small, and our culture—our music—was starting to reflect those changes. By the time we reached the century's halfway mark, Mary's little lamb had turned into a lion. And he was getting ready to roar.

Chuck Berry

The Drifters

Buddy Holly and The Crickets

Elvis Presley

CHAPTER 2

The floodgates open during the 1950s

When Rock Started to Roll

One day, sometime during the 1950s, the sky opened up and a voice boomed, "Let there be Elvis Presley. He shall cause the young people to dance and scream and anger their parents. And while we're at it, let there be Little Richard, too."

Rock & roll was such a profound change from what had come before that it sometimes seems like it dropped down from above (though the older generation may have figured it came from below). Of course, music never really appears from out of the blue. Rock & roll wasn't just revolutionary—it was *evolutionary*.

Not long before the dawn of the rock & roll era, Mom and Dad had been listening to popular music that was rich in vocal harmony. Records by the Mills Brothers, the Ames Brothers and the Ink Spots were selling well, with many of these groups marking the initial crossover of black artists into the white mainstream. Because the fledgling music industry was getting behind the style with big bucks and promotional support, vocal music began to diversify and produce offspring. The Ink Spots begat the Ravens; the Ravens begat the Clovers. With all of this begatting, something was about to be got!

Around the middle of the century, a

ROCK & ROLL WASN'T JUST REVOLUTIONARY —IT WAS EVOLUTIONARY.

subtle but substantial change came to the latest generation of vocal artists. Their songs were injected with a dose of rhythm. Beginning faintly, as if coming from a great distance, it first entered in the form of gentle thumps from the rhythm section. The beat gradually grew louder and more pronounced in the grooves of '50s records. Harmonies that had floated gently and pleasantly were now grounded with a drummer's stomp on his bass-drum pedal. The beat added life and energy, like a fast-beating heart. It quickened the pulse of the music and of the listener. The beat was the sound of youth.

A Sign at the Crossroads

Young people could hear it, too, and they recognized this musical heartbeat as their own. It wasn't heard over the radio just yet—the airwaves still belonged to their parents—but the nation's teenagers started to stir to the music they heard in record stores, at their friends' houses, and on the occasional well-placed jukebox.

The music had a fresh sound, yet every new artist and every new song could be traced back to the recent past. Rock & roll emerged at the crossroads of several styles, and you can look back down each of those intersecting roads

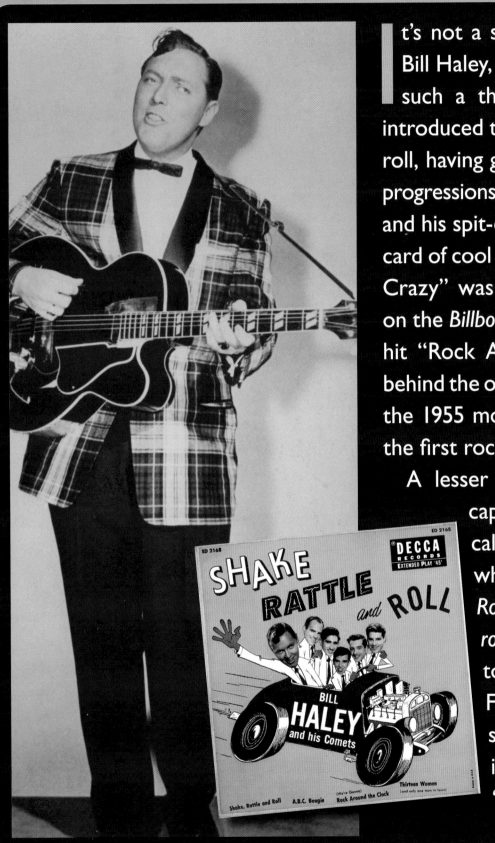

I t's not a stretch to say that without Bill Haley, there may never have been such a thing as rock & roll. Haley introduced the sound of R&B to rock & roll, having given rhythm & blues chord progressions a rhythmic kick in the pants, and his spit-curl hairdo became a calling card of cool late in the '50s. "Crazy Man Crazy" was the first rock & roll song on the *Billboard* charts, and the rousting hit "Rock Around the Clock"—heard behind the opening and closing credits of the 1955 movie *Blackboard Jungle*—was the first rocker to top the charts.

A lesser known feather in Haley's cap is that he'd written a tune called "Rock-a-Beatin' Boogie" which opened with the lyric *Rock rock rock everybody / Roll roll roll everybody*. According to legend, radio legend Alan Freed was crazy about the song—which gave him the idea to start using the phrase "rock & roll" on the air.

BOBBY DARIN

Bobby Darin with George Burns

Versatile vocalist Bobby Darin became a '50s teen idol with "Splish Splash" and "Dream Lover." He moved into Sinatra's territory with "Mack the Knife," which nabbed a Grammy. Darin enjoyed a string of hits and movie roles in the early '60s, reinventing his sound again with the Top 10 folkie hit "If I Were a Carpenter" in 1966.

to see what had come before. Doo wop artists like the Platters and Frankie Lymon & the Teenagers followed vocal groups like the Larks and the Ravens. Rockabilly came predominantly from country, bluegrass, and "hillbilly" music, so guys like Carl Perkins, Buddy Holly, Bill Haley, Jerry Lee Lewis, and Elvis Presley were formed in the image of Jimmie Rodgers, Bill Monroe of the Original Bluegrass Band, and Tennessee Ernie Ford, who was playing hillbilly boogie. Rhythm & blues was exactly what the name implies—blues music infused with rhythm—and in the new generation you could hear the music of artists like Blind Lemon Jefferson and Louis Jordan being updated by the Orioles ("Crying in the Chapel"), the Chords ("Sh-Boom"), and Fats Domino ("Ain't That a Shame"). Even gospel and soul music, with age-old origins in the church, were reborn as rock and soul in artists like the Clovers ("Don't You Know I Love You") and Ray Charles ("I Got a Woman"). Right at the point where all those reborn styles merged—where doo wop, rockabilly, gospel, and rhythm & blues crossed paths—is where rock & roll put up its first signposts.

Brother Ray, in fact, is a great example of how early rock & rollers blurred the lines between styles. "The Genius," as Ray was sometimes known, brought together gospel, blues, soul, country, and rhythm & blues. Bill Haley was one of the first to cross R&B with country & western; Chubby Checker mixed pop and R&B; Elvis blended hillbilly with gospel; and Gene Vincent merged rockabilly and doo wop. They say good composers borrow and great composers steal, and you can find many examples of rock & rollers pickpocketing other styles to enrich their repertoire. As two early examples, Little Richard modeled "Tutti Frutti" on a novelty jazz number by a '30s duo known as Slim and Slam (whose original version had lyrics that were so downright *blue*, I could never have put it on the air. Little Richard scrubbed "Tutti" clean); and Chuck Berry's first big song, "Maybellene," had its origins in an old fiddle tune. Oh, Maybellene! Why can't you be true?

Keepers of the Gate

Rock & roll embodied the twentieth century's great youth movement. On that pivot point the nation turned its

Clyde McPhatter

He led the Drifters to fame with his high tenor voice, then launched a solo career, hitting the pop charts with "A Lover's Question" and "Treasure of Love." McPhatter paved the way for singers like Smokey Robinson and Sam Cooke to cross over to pop audiences.

ELViS PRESLeY

There's no doubt in my mind that if it weren't for the man pictured here, I wouldn't be writing this book. Elvis Presley was the first person to shift all of the pieces of the rock & roll puzzle into place, in the process giving rise to an entire industry. In him we saw the culmination of music, image, and attitude. He was a handsome rebel with good manners, breaking the hearts of teenaged girls while charming their moms at the same time. The sexual energy he exuded in early television appearances was fueled by fiery rhythms and suggestive hip swinging—which infuriated censors but sent ratings through the roof.

Elvis's mythic status often overshadows his musical contributions: He really broke as much ground through song as he did as an icon of pop culture. Elvis was the one who

Sure, he was the King, but Elvis started out as a pawn. Just like you and me.

first fused country and blues to create rockabilly, and no one was more influential in bringing the black sound of R&B to white audiences. Throughout his career he would also integrate elements of pop, gospel (an influence from his early churchgoing days), and bluegrass—all amounting to the musical gumbo that is the essence of rock & roll.

He kick-started rock & roll culture, and you can choose among any of several points to identify the "start" of the Elvis Presley phenomenon: in the Tupelo, Mississippi shotgun shack where he was born; when he won $5 in a music contest at the age of eight; at the Sun Records studio where he made his first recording, a cover of the Ink Spots' "My Happiness" for his mother; or in January 1956 when he recorded his first hit, "Heartbreak Hotel," in a Nashville studio.

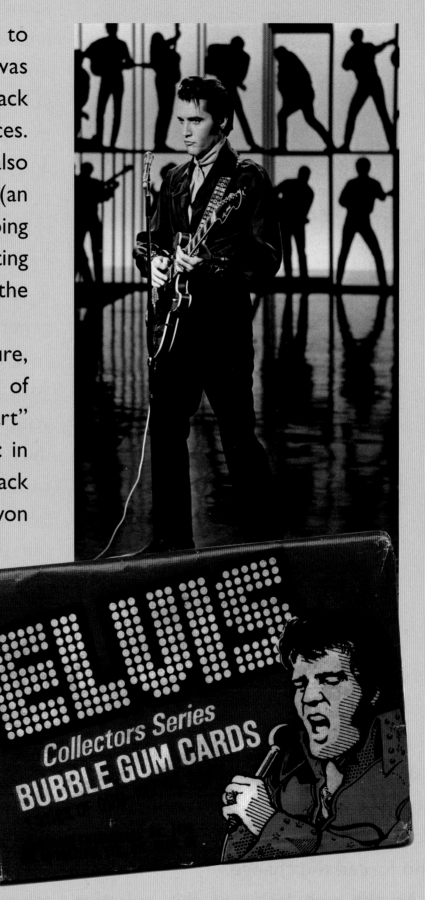

From out of a black-and-white landscape leaped a population of colorful new role models.

perspective toward the young, and it's never turned away. To this day, America takes all of its cultural cues from the twenty-five-and-under crowd. The irony, though—and you don't hear this too often—is that it was the older generation who forced the change.

As the popularity of this pulsating new rock & roll music started to grow, some very smart radio broadcasters and record industry executives took notice. They picked up on its appeal and started testing its commercial viability by spinning more records on the air and signing more artists to recording contracts. The captains of industry recognized quickly that there was immense untapped potential in rock & roll, even as many members of their generation derided it as "rot and roll."

It took someone in the adult world with keen ears and a vision of the youth market's potential to adapt the music for commercial markets and catapult it into the mainstream. Young people throughout time have been our dreamers and our poets—but not our marketeers. Without the bucks behind them, without the hype, without someone burning the coals of industry, young artists would never have the steam to gain locomotion. The people who drive the train are the tough-edged elders who already have miles behind them.

Young people are the risk takers, and the 1950s produced a flood of teenagers taking a chance on new music. But

Frankie Lymon + the Teenagers

Hailing from the hard streets of New York City, these doo wop stars were first heard in the hallways of the buildings they lived in. One neighbor asked them to put music to a love letter he'd written, yielding their debut hit, "Why Do Fools Fall in Love." In 1956, Frankie Lymon was just thirteen years old, and the rest of the guys only sixteen, when "Fools" sold 100,000 copies in three weeks.

Frankie Avalon

A teen idol with a voice to match his looks, Frankie Avalon had thirty-one hit singles—thirty-one!—from 1958 to 1962, including "Just Ask Your Heart," "Venus," and "Bobby Sox to Stockings." In the '60s Avalon got into the movies, chasing Annette Funicello through the surf in beach-party movies and playing a few dramatic roles as well.

Frankie Avalon with Dick Clark

Buddy Holly and The Crickets

The DNA of rock & roll's "beat" groups (like the Beatles) can be traced to this well-loved Texan, who provided the prototype for the performing songwriter, the electric-guitar-playing frontman, and the shy guy with a heart of gold. Born Charles Hardin Holley, the Buddy we came to know and love first hit the big time with "That'll Be the Day" in 1957. Holly's other early hits with the Crickets, including "Peggy Sue" and "Maybe Baby," were neatly wrapped morsels of poppy goodness. One reason it hurt so badly to lose Buddy Holly in that infamous plane crash was that we were so certain he had a long career ahead. He was just twenty-three years old when he was lost, with tour mates Ritchie Valens and J. P. "The Big Bopper" Richardson, in February of 1959.

The quartet pictured on this posthumous 1962 release includes Buddy, Joe B. Mauldin (bass), Jerry Allison (drums), and Niki Sullivan, who left the band in 1957 (rhythm guitar)

Jerry Lee Lewis

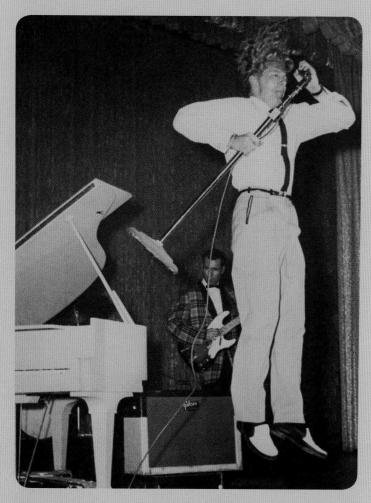

Piano-pounding wild man Jerry Lee Lewis scored huge '50s hits with the boogie-woogie rockers "Whole Lotta Shakin' Going On" and "Great Balls of Fire." Hell-bent on upstaging Chuck Berry at an Alan Freed show in '58, "The Killer" torched his piano, belting out "Great Balls of Fire" as it burned.

someone has to open the floodgate. It's a big, heavy door, and it takes someone very powerful to swing it open.

Heroes for Sale!

Before long it became clear that rock & roll was not just a sound, but a look and an attitude. Radio was teaching us more and more about the young players, newspapers started to print reasonably favorable reviews, and the faces of artists started to appear on the television. To capitalize on the trend and carry it headlong into the public view, a wave of teen magazines hit the nation's newsstands. In the glossy pages of *Hit Parader, Teen Pin-Ups,* and *Movieland*, rock & rollers were transformed from musicians into heroes.

A new population of heroes, and not just idols, was exactly what the youth wanted and needed. The older generation had their General MacArthurs and President Eisenhowers to toe the conservative line. Consider, for a moment, that the adults of the 1950s were conservative in the truest sense. They conserved everything. Kids would snicker as their parents left a restaurant stuffing their pockets with sugar packets

THE DRIFTERS

Within the smooth-as-silk harmonies of the Drifters, summer loving could just as easily be found "Under the Boardwalk" as "Up on the Roof." The legendary group brought doo wop into the mainstream with thirteen chart hits, many of which remain staples of pop radio today.

CONNIE FRANCIS

Concetta Rosa Maria Franconero wasn't yet twenty years old when her father convinced her to record a song he loved from 1923. "Who's Sorry Now" shot her to the top of the charts in 1958, where she remained for the next five years. Connie was a chameleon, and she could just as easily please the oldies crowd as sing to a rockabilly beat ("Everybody's Somebody's Fool," which went to number 1), try a mariachi sound ("My Heart Has a Mind of Its Own," also number 1), or join the kids cruising the streets with "Where the Boys Are" and the bouncing "Stupid Cupid."

and leftover dinner rolls. But it was a way of life they had learned the hard way, having been children of the Great Depression and survivors of the Second World War. They wanted to keep what they had because they knew too well the pain of losing everything. The threat of communism left many fearful that all they'd worked for might once again be stripped away. For mid-twentieth-century parents, conservatism was not just a way of life but a way of survival. But for their kids, it looked like a life that was stamped from a restricting, petrified mold—and that mold was due to be shattered.

From out of this black-and-white landscape leaped a population of colorful new role models, the champions of the next generation. Kids struggling against the old guard watched in empathy as James Dean writhed under his father's weight in *East of Eden*. Teenaged boys were fixed in front of mirrors, working on their Marlon Brando poses and trying to replicate Bill Haley's spit-curl on their own heads of hair. Teenaged girls took their tips from movie stars, trying

ROCK & ROLL CULTURE SENT A SHOCKWAVE THROUGH THE GENERATIONS.

to match Audrey Hepburn's grace with Marilyn Monroe's homespun sex appeal. Flipping the pages of *Photoplay* magazine, they squealed at the notion of winning that dream date with Fabian.

And of course, at the center of it all, there was Elvis Presley. The King of Rock & Roll crossed all the available media, selling hit records, appearing on magazine covers, starring in films, and ruling the radio. He bucked tradition by doing what he wanted, when he wanted

> It took someone in the adult world to catapult young people's music into the mainstream.

—though not without a polite tip of his hat to the ladies in the room. A key to his appeal was that teenagers felt they could relate to him. He came from so little, born in a shotgun shack to poor parents in East Tupelo, Mississippi. Sure, he was the King, but Elvis started out as a pawn. Just like you and me. Behind his grandiose success and loud rock & rolling was a whispered message: *You can do this, too. You can live your dreams.*

Fashion, attitude, style, and even a dictionary's worth of lingo were all pieces of the rock & roll puzzle (you with me, cool cats?). Without each one in place, the whole picture would never have become visible. The new heroes beautified the rock & roll generation and provided an identity for young people—and, at the same time, they helped the older generation identify a massive new marketplace. As far as the youth were concerned, they were living a carefree life based on creativity and rebellion. Meanwhile, some wise elders recognized the movement as a potent commercial industry. Between the two was a yin-yang relationship that worked for both sides: Young people wanted a new aesthetic, and older people wanted

Sam Cooke

The incomparable Cooke was a study in contrasts. He started as a gospel singer, yet every song that flowed from him sounded romantic. He had a raspy quality in his throat, yet his voice was the essence of smooth. Sam also drew both black and white fans in huge numbers, appealing to R&B and pop audiences alike. His song "A Change Is Gonna Come" was a Civil Rights anthem—but, sadly, was also a posthumous hit in 1965, as he had been gunned down a year before at the age of thirty-three. The woman who killed him told the court that Sam's final, shocked words were, "Lady…you shot me."

Gene Vincent and His Blue Caps

An early rock & roll rebel, Gene Vincent entered the music business after leaving the Navy, where he had severely damaged one of his legs in a motorcycle accident. Expertly blending rockabilly with doo wop, Gene Vincent and his Blue Caps (who really did wear blue caps) scored a big hit with "Be-Bop-a-Lula" in 1956.

to sell it to them. It may sound crassly capitalistic to say it, but the reality is that commercialization is based on a time-proven formula: Aesthetics + Exploitation = Success. And the formula was working well on both sides of the equation.

Who's Sorry Now?

Rock & roll culture sent a shockwave through the generations. For the first few years, the older generation cried foul: Church ladies thought that rock & roll was the devil's music, and parents promised it would grow hair on your hands. But once they recovered from their astonishment, something unprecedented happened. Mom and Dad started to dig rock & roll.

By the late 1950s, the youth movement had become so powerful and sophisticated that the adult world saw fit to join the club. It was a first for everybody. Looking back to the flappers of the 1920s and the big band swingers of the '30s and '40s, the social scene had belonged exclusively to adults—the young 'uns had no culture of their own to speak of. But now this youthful music, which was eventually to become an

FATS DOMINO

New Orleans pianist Antoine "Fats" Domino had the first million-seller in rock history with 1949's "The Fat Man" on Imperial Records. He climbed the pop charts in 1955 with "Ain't That a Shame" and his piano style reportedly inspired Paul McCartney's "Lady Madonna." Domino and his family were rescued by the Coast Guard after Hurricane Katrina. Fats still lives and performs in his beloved New Orleans.

You can find many examples of rock + rollers pickpocketing other styles to enrich their repertoire.

international language accepted all over the globe, was shared with the grown-up world.

Remember that the older generation was no stranger to vocal music, which preceded doo wop. Parents were attuned to those harmonies. Though the big beat was something new to get used to, you could catch people over forty tapping their foot under the table. Plus, a number of artists who were hitting the teen pop charts had emerged from musical styles and even from singing groups that the older generation had admired. Jackie Wilson came out of the Dominoes, Clyde McPhatter from the Drifters, and Sam Cooke from the Soul Stirrers. Connie Francis was not so far

afield from the more familiar Doris Day, if endowed with a little more sway and swagger. Young Johnny Cash still had a foot planted in good ol' country music. Maybe the strange new world was not so strange or new after all.

The music of the 1950s was like a giant magnet. It had an incredibly strong pull. Once you stopped fighting it, you were stuck for good.

Still, for the adults, rock & roll was a phenomenon to watch with a wary eye. For the new generation, it was the focal point of their optimism, their rebellion, and their hope for the future. It was a movement empowered by millions. Society was about to break loose like it never had before.

Chuck Berry

Music historians have said that Chuck Berry would have been crowned the king of rock & roll in the 1950s had it not been for America's deep racial divides at the time. Berry was good looking, he was a polished performer (marked by his sharp suits, onstage banter, and patented "duck walk"), and he played guitar like he was ringin' a bell. His long string of classic rock & roll hits was kicked off with "Maybellene"—a name Berry took not from a philandering femme fatale, but from a brand of hair cream!

The Everly Brothers

The closely paired vocals of Don and Phil Everly established a standard for harmony singing that many have strived for and few have achieved. Part country, part rockabilly, part rock & roll, these Kentucky brothers deserved every ounce of the superstardom they garnered beginning in the late '50s. However, there were unsung heroes behind the hits, too: the husband-wife songwriting team of Boudleaux and Felice Bryant penned the Everlys' first smash, "Bye Bye Love," and helped cement their success with "Wake Up Little Susie," "All I Have to Do Is Dream," and "Devoted to You."

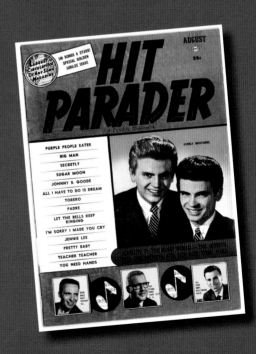

COUSIN BRUCIE'S HONOR ROLL

Rock & Roll Pioneers of the 1950s

It's just about impossible to pinpoint a moment in time when rock & roll began. But beginning in the 1950s, adventuresome artists started mixing together older musical traditions such as blues, doo wop, country, and gospel to create a whole new sound. Included here are just a few of the artists who were there at the start of the rock & roll era. I'm naming forty of them here—there are probably another 400 that deserve mention! Rock & roll is a long road, and we honor all of the travelers along its path. **Cousins, this list is alphabetical!**

Lee Andrews and the Hearts	Bo Diddley	Little Richard
Paul Anka	Dion and the Belmonts	Frankie Lymon & the Teenagers
Frankie Avalon	Fats Domino	Clyde McPhatter
LaVerne Baker	The Drifters	Ricky Nelson
Harry Belafonte	Duane Eddy	Roy Orbison
Chuck Berry	The Everly Brothers	Carl Perkins
James Brown	The Five Satins	The Platters
Johnny Cash	Connie Francis	Elvis Presley
Chubby Checker	Bill Haley and His Comets	Smokey Robinson & the Miracles
The Coasters	Buddy Holly and the Crickets	Bobby Rydell
Eddie Cochran	The Kingston Trio	Neil Sedaka
Sam Cooke	Brenda Lee	The Shirelles
Danny and the Juniors	Jerry Lee Lewis	Gene Vincent
Bobby Darin	Little Anthony & the Imperials	Jackie Wilson

The Beach Boys

The Ronettes

Roy Orbison

Smokey Robinson & the Miracles

CHAPTER 3

The early 1960s

The Great Melting Pot

I've had the good fortune to know a great many musicians in my time, and it's led me to a few conclusions that I would like to share with you here. Clearly I have great respect for them—after all, I've dedicated my career to what these artists create. But I've also been impressed with their respect for one another.

People often look at others and make judgments based on some simple observations. What are his politics? How was he brought up and what education does he have? How is he dressed? Does he smell okay?

But when one musician considers another, all of that is very secondary. They instead consider the music and the aesthetic experience. They listen to the person and breathe that person in. With their great insight, the things that set many other people apart simply evaporate. Racial distinctions, class differences, and social judgments all go right out the window. You can meet a lot of musical masters who are *way* off base socially, sure, and there are also some bigots in the bunch. (Nope, I ain't telling.) But there seems to be this innate respect among players. Can you even imagine someone like Keith Richards looking down his nose at a black man?

The Beach Boys

The Beach Boys had such a mellow, laid back image that it's easy to underestimate how much work went into crafting their sound. But there's no denying how influential they were in the history of rock & roll. With Brian Wilson at the helm, these guys could never have faded

into the Southern California landscape. Four and a half decades after they first entered the charts with "Surfin' Safari" in 1962, the perfection of their work still resonates with listeners all over the world in dozens of hits including "I Get Around," "Help Me, Rhonda," "Barbara Ann," "Surfer Girl," "Good Vibrations," "God Only Knows" and "Caroline No." Music luminaries from Bob Dylan and Paul McCartney to Stevie Wonder and Leonard Bernstein have bowed in reverence to the Beach Boys' talent.

Fast cars, high surf, and pretty girls provided the subject matter for their greatest hits, yet there was always far more to Wilson's creativity than teenybopper appeal. From the very first days, he and the Boys had sought to update the precise vocal harmonies of the Four Freshmen (look 'em up!) with the rompin' rock & roll sound being made famous by Chuck Berry. Wilson, who had written most of the group's songs, unleashed the full potential of his composing and producing chops in 1966 with *Pet Sounds*, widely hailed as the greatest rock album ever.

DION

Dion (center) & the Belmonts

Originally staking his claim to fame as the leader of Dion & the Belmonts, who fused doo wop and rock, Dion DiMucci matured well beyond the style made famous on "I Wonder Why" and "Teenager in Love." Dion emerged as a solo artist in 1960 and scored big with "The Wanderer" and "Runaround Sue." After battling some personal demons—and beating them soundly—Dion rose again as an artist exploring Christian themes and genuinely bluesy moods.

The Crystals

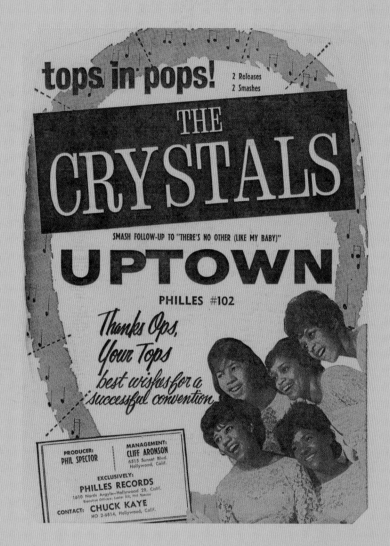

tops in pops! 2 Releases 2 Smashes

THE CRYSTALS

SMASH FOLLOW-UP TO "THERE'S NO OTHER (LIKE MY BABY)"

UPTOWN

PHILLES #102

Thanks Ops, Your Tops best wishes for a successful convention

| PRODUCER: PHIL SPECTOR | MANAGEMENT: CLIFF ARONSON 6515 Sunset Blvd. Hollywood, Calif. |

EXCLUSIVELY: PHILLES RECORDS 1610 North Argyle—Hollywood 28, Calif.

CONTACT: CHUCK KAYE HO 2-6814, Hollywood, Calif.

This girl group sensation from the early '60s hit it big with singles like "He's a Rebel," "Da Doo Ron Ron" and "Uptown." A socially conscious group, the Crystals are also remembered for their ballad of domestic abuse called "He Hit Me (And It Felt Like a Kiss)."

He built his life around the blues and Chuck Berry!

Not to get too political about all of this, but my point is that rock & roll music from the very start has been a great model for democracy. In the musician's eyes—or let's say in the musician's *ears*—there is no skin color, no judgment. Music is a reflection of the times, and not the other way around, but in rock & roll we saw artists shining a light toward a brighter future. It would turn out to be a defining difference of the 1960s.

The Universal Language

As our nation grew smaller and more tightly knit, thanks to advances in communication, the diverse cultures within America started sampling one another. National and regional radio broadcasts, plus the widening availability of records, made it simpler for someone in Kansas to eavesdrop on music to the north, south, east, and west.

Down south we had rockabilly, the midwest had rhythm & blues, and the northeast had doo wop artists galore. In the early 1960s, the west coast had the beginnings of surf music in artists like Dick Dale and the Deltones and, of course, the Beach Boys. By way of radio and records, though, all of the landlocked states were offered a glimpse of the ocean. The only water a kid in Des Moines, Iowa, might have seen was in his bathtub once a week—but suddenly he could "see" a breaking wave when he heard "Surfin' Safari."

Rock & roll provided the common ground for people to start sharing sounds and ideas. For example, take a real foreign-sounding style like calypso. Hearing a purebred calypso rhythm would give most Americans a twitch in their eye. But sweetened and softened by Harry Belafonte, "Day-O (the Banana Boat Song)" and "Jamaica Farewell" went down smoothly. Same goes for rockabilly artists like Carl Perkins, Jerry Lee Lewis, and Buddy Holly, who spun hillbilly grit into palatable rockers like "Blue Suede Shoes," "Breathless," and "Not Fade Away." Ben E. King tapped pure soul and blues to give us "Stand By Me" and Etta James drew on gospel for "At Last."

It's like learning a foreign language. When you first start, you cling to the familiar sounds and words. As your

Lesley Gore

Lesley Gore, one of the true sweethearts of rock & roll, is best known for her 1963 pop hit "It's My Party," which she recorded when she was only sixteen. Lesley followed up with several others— many produced by Quincy Jones, the man who helped put her on the map—including "Judy's Turn to Cry" and "You Don't Own Me." To this day, Lesley appears in clubs and concert halls to standing-room-only audiences. She's a true star.

Smokey Robinson & the Miracles

The 1960s were the golden age of the Miracles, bookended on one side with "Shop Around" in 1960 and at the other with "Tears of a Clown" in 1970. In the years between, fans were treated to the romantic hits of this post–doo wop quintet, with miraculous numbers including "You've Really Got a Hold on Me," "Ooo Baby Baby," "The Tracks of My Tears," and "Going to a Go Go." Taking nothing away from the dynamite vocalists doing a smooth two-step behind their mic stands, the group also served as the main vehicle for the songwriting talent of their frontman, Smokey Robinson.

Singing sweet and high, Smokey was a lady-killer from the very first— and apparently his magic worked on one-time Miracle Claudette Rogers, who married him in 1963. But when Berry Gordy, Jr. first brought Smokey aboard his fledgling Motown recording label, Gordy knew he was doing more than signing a singer. He was grooming a second-in-charge, arming his label with star power, and securing the future success of his business. Once the Miracles hit, Smokey started lending his songwriting and production talents to the Motown roster, including the likes of Mary Wells, the Supremes, and, perhaps most famously, the Temptations. It was Smokey who etched a place in history for the Temps by writing and producing songs like

"The Way You Do the Things You Do" (by Smokey and Miracle Bobby Rogers), "My Girl" (by Smokey and Miracle Ronnie White), and "Get Ready" (that one was all Smokey). Music historians love to repeat Bob Dylan's praise of Smokey Robinson: The guy many consider rock & roll's greatest songwriter called Robinson "America's greatest living poet."

No one understood the value of crossover appeal better than Berry Gordy, Jr., the visionary behind Motown Records.

comfort level grows, your ear gets more sophisticated, and before you know it you're chatting it up with the locals. The rock & roll beat gave us this huge comfort zone in which to try out all sorts of foreign sounds. It was an interpretation everyone could understand. As these diverse styles crossed over into rock & roll, we started sharing and enjoying the poetry of different cultures.

One sweep through the greatest hits of the early 1960s proves how artists were drawing on multicultural sources—some of them from the international community and some from our own backyard. You could hear the worldly influences in chart toppers like Ben E. King's "Spanish Harlem," with its marimba part and vocal ornaments, and in "The Lion Sleeps Tonight" by the Tokens, a remake of the Weavers' 1951 hit "Wimoweh." The Weavers, in fact, had remade their own hit from an older South African song called "Mbube," and mispronounced the original African lyric *uyimbube* (meaning "you're a lion") in their version.

The adaptation of influences from a broad variety of American cultures makes the same point over and over again. "Big Bad John" by Jimmy Dean echoed the influences of coal-mining states, and Sam Cooke's "A Change Is Gonna Come" had the underpinnings of

John Fitzgerald Kennedy

John Fitzgerald Kennedy, at forty-three, remains the youngest president ever elected, and his 1961 inauguration kicked off the youth-crazy 1960s. Kennedy steered the country safely through the Cuban Missile Crisis, created the Peace Corps, railed against the Berlin wall ("Ich bin ein Berliner!"), started the Apollo Project to put a man on the moon, and proposed the legislation that became the Civil Rights Act of 1964. Of course, he was only human, and his judgment most infamously lapsed with the Bay of Pigs. He also escalated American involvement in the fight between North and South Vietnam, although he was leaning toward troop withdrawal at the time of his shocking motorcade assassination in Dallas—a pivotal event that is painfully burned into the memory of every American old enough to hear the terrible news on November 22, 1963. The loss of Kennedy marked a turn in our history. Nearly half a century later we still haven't found our way back to Camelot.

Inspired by Gandhi, Baptist minister Martin Luther King, Jr. built the Civil Rights movement on the principle of nonviolent resistance, leading marches and boycotts in then-segregated Jim Crow towns like Birmingham and Selma. MLK was so incredibly energetic and charismatic—when he got in front of a microphone, he was easily as powerful as any rock & roll star. With his unforgettable "I Have a Dream" speech at the March on Washington in 1963, King galvanized the largest crowd of protesters that had ever assembled in our nation's Capitol. And the rest of the nation heard them. The Civil Rights Act in 1964 and the Voting Rights Act in 1965 were inked thanks in large part to King, and in 1964 he became the youngest person to win the Nobel Peace Prize.

It's still heartbreaking that a star as bright as his could be snuffed out by an assassin's bullet. But his spirit lives on as a light leading us through the darkness toward peace and brotherhood.

deep gospel from the South. "Ring of Fire," Johnny Cash's ode to burnin' love, was straight out of country & western culture but also featured a Mexican mariachi horn section, and the Beach Boys' 1963 smash "Be True to Your School" was pure *teenage* culture. Each one had its roots in a unique style—but every one is pure rock & roll.

Sweet as Syrup

Familiarity and comfort were the core ingredients of rock & roll, and that fact did not go unnoticed by the growing music industry. The packaging, marketing, and sale of rock & roll depended on a music that sounded new and edgy—but not *too* new or so edgy that it estranged the listeners at its base.

The industry had to craft rock & roll idols in the image of heroes who were already proven and accepted. As anyone in marketing can tell you, the most perilous thing you can do is make an abrupt change to a known quantity. The perfect example sits on your breakfast table every time you have pancakes. Many of us remember the Aunt Jemima icon of the '50s, a dark-skinned black woman with chubby cheeks and a red

Thanks to radio and records, a landlocked kid in Des Moines, Iowa, could "see" a breaking wave when he heard "Surfin' Safari."

kerchief on her head—not a far cry from the slave stereotype that originally depicted her fifty years before. But following a few more makeovers, she lost the headgear, her features narrowed, and she acquired a more

LEE GORDON presents

Chubby Checker's TWIST party

Chubby Checker

Chubby Checker taught America how to do "The Twist" with his 1960 cover of Hank Ballard's R&B hit. "The Twist" remains one of the most popular singles of all time. Although Checker initially felt frustrated at being typecast as a dance artist, he cut a succession of dance hits and won a Grammy in 1961 for "Let's Twist Again." Checker got not only teens, but their parents, out on the dance floor twisting the night away—putting a stake in formal dancing and ushering in the rock & roll era.

BRENDA LEE

"Little Miss Dynamite" had the throaty belt of a seasoned rocker by the time she turned twelve. The delectable and deceptively diminutive Lee sold over 100 million records, from the Nashville tearjerker "I'm Sorry" and hard-rocking "Dynamite" to the holiday classic "Rockin' Around the Christmas Tree." Brenda Lee charted in more music categories than any other woman in recording history.

contemporary style. Before we knew it, Aunt Jemima looked like a TV talk-show host!

Likewise, rock & roll of the 1960s would never have succeeded if the purist styles behind it—blues, gospel, R&B—hadn't been homogenized. It had to be comfortable for the listeners of the day. Remember the rockabilly artist Sleepy LaBeef? No, you don't, and that's just the point, because Sleepy was plenty talented but a little too pure for the mainstream: not enough *rocka* and a little too much *billy*. Don't tell him I said that, though, because Sleepy was about six-foot-seven and once played The Swamp Thing in a horror movie (1968's *The Exotic Ones*).

Hitsville

No one understood the value of crossover appeal better than Berry Gordy, Jr., the visionary behind Motown Records. Without the guidance of Berry Gordy, the world would never have heard the passionate, moving music of well-loved artists like Smokey Robinson, Marvin Gaye, Michael Jackson, Diana Ross, and Stevie Wonder.

Gordy was from Detroit, the Motor

NEIL SEDAKA

Neil Sedaka was as big a hit behind the scenes as he was behind the microphone. As one of the most successful songwriters to come out of New York's Brill Building, a breeding ground for some of the world's finest pop composers, my Brooklyn buddy Neil paired up with lyricist Howard Greenfield to write hits including "Where the Boys Are" and "Stupid Cupid" for Connie Francis. While other clean-cut solo singers had faded by the late 1950s, Sedaka had a series of hits for himself including "The Diary" (inspired by Connie Francis' own diary, which she wouldn't let Neil read), "Happy Birthday, Sweet Sixteen," and "Calendar Girl." He also wrote "Oh! Carol" for his ex-girlfriend and fellow Brill Building star Carole King. Only a handful of artists have ever topped the charts with two different versions of the same composition, as Neil did: "Breaking Up Is Hard to Do" reached number 1 as an upbeat hit in 1962, and was remade as a ballad in 1975. It hit number 8 the following year.

LITTLE DEVIL

By
NEIL SEDAKA
HOWARD GREENFIELD

Recorded by
NEIL SEDAKA
on
RCA VICTOR
Records

Price 60¢

02358

ALDON MUSIC INC.—NEVINS—KIRSHNER ASSOCIATES, INC.
Sole Selling Agents:
keys - hansen, inc.
119 W. 57th St., NEW YORK 19, N.Y.

The Shirelles

These Passaic, New Jersey teenagers first hit the charts with their own song, "I Met Him on a Sunday." A tune penned by Carole King and Gerry Goffin, though, took them to new heights. In 1960, "Will You Still Love Me Tomorrow" became the first record by a black female group to reach number 1. To many, the Shirelles perfected the girl-group sound.

City, and had a deep appreciation for the kind of blues, gospel, R&B, and soul that was being pumped out on labels including Chess Records (Muddy Waters, Willie Dixon) and Stax Records (Wilson Pickett, Sam and Dave). But he knew in his heart of hearts that to help black artists who were really struggling to get out of the antiquated "race records" genre, he had to shift these players onto the white audience's playing field.

Gordy formed an organization that taught these artists how to walk, talk, dance, and sing. He dressed them in suits, styled their hair, and softened the edges on their record productions. He preserved their artistry but cherry-picked their music to cater to the broadest common denominator.

In anyone else's hands, that would have resulted in a watering down that neither the artists nor the audience would tolerate. But Gordy adapted the black musician's experience for the mainstream audience with taste and precision, and made them into superstars.

With early smashes like "The One Who Really Loves You" (Mary Wells), "Shop Around" (The Miracles),

Marvin Gaye

The Prince of Soul proved with his brilliant 1971 concept album *What's Going On* that R&B fans were ready for sophisticated jazz-tinged fare that grappled with the issues of the day. The million-dollar deal Gaye negotiated with Warner after its success made him the highest paid black artist of the day. He proved he was worth every cent with his sensual smash album *Let's Get It On*. Marvin began his solo career after his doo wop group, the Moonglows, which disbanded in 1960. While Marvin's music has long been a favorite for late-night plays on bedroom stereos, it was also deeply infused with themes of social and environmental awareness.

"Fingertips" (Stevie Wonder), "Please Mr. Postman" (The Marvelettes), and "Stop! In the Name of Love" (The Supremes)—we could go on all day—Motown Records earned the nickname Hitsville, USA. It wasn't Hitsville Midwest or Hitsville Detroit. Gordy made the music of America.

What was so compelling that it pulled British musicians three thousand miles across the Atlantic Ocean?

Meanwhile, Across the Pond...

This art form of rock & roll—and I insist on calling it an art form—is the first popular music ever to become truly international. It reaches through every boundary. If you play it in Japan, China, Russia, or Uzbekistan, it'll get to every young person that listens to music. In fact, you don't even have to be young, just young at heart.

Without the USA even knowing it, rock & roll had permeated the borders of the United Kingdom as early as the 1950s. In the pubs of London and in social halls across the countryside, the American beat was resonating with British youth. An English disc jockey by the name of John Peel was championing a whole roster of British rock & roll bands, and every so often a record would arrive from across the pond from a group that was reportedly causing a stir. The R&B outfit Manfred Mann was big on the London club scene, and Cliff Richard was topping the UK charts as Britain's answer to Elvis. Some moptops called the Beatles had a tune entitled "Please Please Me," and an early cover of "My Bonnie" was a favorite among

Sean Connery as James Bond

JAMES BOND

"**B**ond…James Bond." You can't say it without thinking of one guy, Sean Connery. You also can't say it without thinking about Ursula Andress in *Dr. No*, and all the other Bond girls to follow. The Cold War was in full swing in 1962 and "secret agents" were poised to capture our imagination. *Dr. No* did that and much more, introducing movie audiences to the debonair and deadly 007, the guy who saved the world repeatedly, with a little help from the latest high-powered gadgetry from Her Majesty's Secret Service. Followed by *From Russia With Love, Goldfinger, Thunderball*, and *You Only Live Twice*, James Bond movies were big-screen entertainment in the 1960s—and still are today, whether you like them shaken or stirred.

Tensions mount in the war room, from the movie, Dr. Strangelove or: How I Learned to Stop Worrying and Love the Bomb

An Open Line between Washington and Moscow

The Cuban Missile Crisis in October of 1962 had been too close a call. At the eleventh hour, President Kennedy and Soviet Premier Nikita Khrushchev had managed to avert nuclear disaster through diplomatic relations, but both sides of the Cold War agreed that they couldn't risk any miscommunications in the future. Getting a message wrong could send the missiles flying.

So, on August 30, 1963, the White House announced that a hotline between the Pentagon and the Kremlin would "help reduce the risk of war occurring by accident or miscalculation." To this day, everyone pictures a red telephone underneath a glass cake cover, like the

one Batman had. But the hotline was actually a string of connections combining land lines and radio paths that relayed a typed message from Washington to London to Copenhagen to Stockholm to Helsinki and *then* to Moscow. Still, a message originating in D.C. could reach Moscow in minutes rather than the hours it took to send an overseas message by telegram. Hey cousins, no tipping the Western Union man!

The hotline was heavily publicized, and provided a little bit of thawing in the Cold War era. It encouraged the idea that the US and the USSR might really see eye to eye—or ear to ear, as the case may be—when the lives of citizens were in the balance.

their local Liverpool fans. But at the time, Top 40 success in England barely made a blip on the radar of American listeners.

The Beatles' first appearance on *The Ed Sullivan Show* in February of 1963 is often regarded as the explosion that heralded the British Invasion. The Fab Four, Herman's Hermits, the Hollies, the Kinks, the Animals, and many other troops were on the front lines, but they didn't just arrive on our shores from nowhere. They were doing training exercises back home well before they loaded up their landing vessels with electric guitars and amplifiers.

A music scene had been developing in England parallel to our own here in America. Many of the young players, including John Lennon, Pete Townshend (the Who), Keith Richards (the Rolling Stones), and Dave Davies (the Kinks), had begun crafting their work in art school, where they learned the power of combining sound and image—a sensibility that would pay off in spades once they hit the States.

Though they were clear across the sea, it's as if these young Brits had been listening to American rock & roll with

The Contours

Berry Gordy, Jr., the man behind Motown Records, was determined to bring the R&B sound to pop and rock audiences. One of his earliest discoveries was the Contours, who helped realize Gordy's dream with the crossover hit "Do You Love Me" in 1962. "Do You Love Me" was also featured in the 1987 film *Dirty Dancing*—just like me! I played the magician who sawed Jennifer Grey in half. Sorry, Baby.

Stevie Wonder

FINGERTIPS - Part 1 & 2

LITTLE STEVIE WONDER THE 12 YEAR OLD

GENIUS

TAMLA RECORDS

54080

To just score a number 1 hit ("Fingertips, Pt. 2") at the age of twelve would have been enough to earn any performer a place in history. To achieve an R&B/pop crossover smash ("Uptight (Everything's Alright)") at age fourteen would have been another. But these were only a few early mile markers in the long, illustrious career of Stevie Wonder.

Stevie was blinded as a newborn—believed to be the result of too much oxygen in his incubator—but no one could ever say the kid lacked vision.

By the age of nine he was a force to be reckoned with on piano, drums, and harmonica. After first being signed to a recording contract, he was marketed in the early days as "the twelve-year-old genius" hoping that audiences would associate Little Stevie with "the Genius," Ray Charles. Of course, Stevie was such a powerhouse in his own right that he never really needed the assist. His talent was simply undeniable, and over time he would show his mastery of many, many styles including R&B, soul, funk, "Tin Pan Alley" pop, jazz, rock, reggae, and "world" music. He had a hit covering Bob Dylan's "Blowin' in the Wind" in 1966, and while hard rock was having its heyday in the late 1960s, Stevie was knocking out timeless gems such as "For Once in My Life" and "My Cherie Amour." Even these songs barely scratched the surface of his talent as a songwriter and musician. The years to come would prove again and again the depth and breadth of Stevie Wonder's talent.

DARLENE LOVE

When Bob B. Soxx and the Blue Jeans had a hit with "Zip-a-Dee-Doo-Dah" in 1963, the woman delivering the charismatic lead vocal was Darlene Love, who also belted out "He's a Rebel" for the Crystals. She has cut out a long and esteemed career that includes two Top 40 hits of her own, "Today I Met the Boy I'm Going to Marry" and "Wait Till my Bobby Gets Home," both produced by Phil Spector. Over the years she has been a first-call backup singer, and crossed media to become an actress, too: She played the role of Trish in all of the *Lethal Weapon* movies, and starred in *Hairspray* on Broadway. Darlene continues to share her big, beautiful voice with adoring audiences, and to me the holidays just wouldn't be the same without hearing her sing, "Christmas (Baby Please Come Home)." I love Ms. Love!

Darlene Love (left) with The Blossoms

Peter, Paul & Mary

This folk trio recorded vocal-driven hits like "Puff the Magic Dragon" and "Leaving on a Jet Plane." The group is also known for performing Pete Seeger's song "If I Had a Hammer" at the '63 March on Washington in which Martin Luther King, Jr. delivered his now-legendary "I Have a Dream" speech. This group represented the spirit of change better than any other before them. They were truly patriotic and always had the best interests of our nation at heart. The trio became quintessential leaders of the peace movement, and their music influenced the social and political views of a generation.

A MUSIC SCENE HAD BEEN DEVELOPING IN ENGLAND PARALLEL TO OUR OWN HERE IN AMERICA.

their ears against the wall. The Rolling Stones could make out the strutting blues of America's South, while the Beatles tipped their ears to the more mellifluous vocal sounds of the Beach Boys and the Shirelles. A young girl named Mary O'Brien (later known as Dusty Springfield) had a fondness for Peggy Lee and Motown's girl groups, and the Hollies were big on the Everly Brothers.

The stateside influences mixed well with British styles of their own making. Most famously, the "Mersey sound" was causing a stir in the city of Liverpool (which sits on the River Mersey in northwest England), home to the Beatles, Gerry and the Pacemakers, and Freddie and the Dreamers. Sometimes known as Merseybeat or just "beat music," the sound fused soul and early rock & roll from the USA with Celtic overtones and the percussion of *skiffle,* a folk style invented by Britain's Lonnie Donegan that was played with washboards, homemade kazoos, and twanging saws. (Like zydeco, skiffle is a type of music that uses just about everything but the kitchen sink—though if you can find a way to play the kitchen sink, that'll work, too.) In the industrial city of Birmingham, the "Brum beat" sound put a rougher edge on Merseybeat, which suited its own rough-and-tumble youth just fine. As in America, various regions in England gave way to musical styles that reflected local culture.

Fanfare for the Common Band

The forces were gathering in Britain. The groups who would break here in the States were those with a real grasp of the rock & roll language. Like all of the artists before them to hit the big time, the Brits who brought something new *and* something familiar to the scene were the ones who would eventually endear themselves to American listeners.

Herman's Hermits, for example, were causing a buzz in the UK well before they topped the American charts. What first made it happen stateside for this Manchester band was the smash "I'm Into Something Good"—which was penned by the songwriting team of Carole King and Gerry Goffin from New York City's legendary Brill Building, home of countless hit songwriters and music companies in the 1950s and 1960s. Uncharacteristically for the Hermits' repertoire, "I'm Into Something Good"

sounded like it was straight out of California—a feel-good, happy-go-lucky song that played easily to American tastes. (Incidentally, Peter Noone, who was often recognized as the Herman of Herman's Hermits, has told me more than once that John Lennon coached his music career. To this day, Noone credits Lennon for his success.)

Another way of saying all of this? The artists who gave themselves over to the rock & roll mainstream are the ones who won our hearts.

But what was it about this rock & roll music—born across the ocean and largely on the back of black artists—that appealed to white, working-class kids from England? What bond was so strong that it pulled them three thousand miles across the Atlantic Ocean?

It all comes back to the dream. Not just the American dream, but the dream of rock & roll. As we know from Elvis, a shaggy kid with grease under his fingernails can grow up to shake the world.

For the kids across the big pond, rock & roll held out a promise that blazed like the torch on the Statue of Liberty.

Theodore Bikel, Judy Collins, and Hootenanny *host Jack Linkletter*

HOOTENANNY

Folk music was big business in the early 1960s—that is, until a group of long haired lads from across the pond "invaded" our shores. *Hootenanny*, which debuted in 1963, was a musical variety television series that showcased many popular folk musicians of the time and was filmed in front of college students. Unfortunately, some 1950s attitudes had not left us and *Hootenanny* is probably best remembered today for refusing to allow Pete Seeger on the show because he was thought to be too left wing. Ridiculous decision of course, but many artists joined in boycotting the show in support of Seeger, and *Hootenanny* ran out of hoot by 1964.

JAN & DEAN

Ollege students Jan Berry and Dean Torrence epitomized the clean-cut yet irreverent California surf culture of the early '60s. The rock duo scored sixteen Top 40 hits, collaborating with the Beach Boys' Brian Wilson on hits like "Surf City," "The Little Old Lady from Pasadena," "Dead Man's Curve," and "Baby Talk."

MARY WELLS

Often regarded as one of the leaders in the black music movement, Mary Wells was nicknamed "The First Lady of Motown." She recorded a string of hits that often built on her collaboration with Smokey Robinson. Her signature smash "My Guy" echoes on the airwaves for all time.

The Marvelettes

The Marvelettes paved the way for their Motown sisters like Martha and the Vandellas as well as the Supremes. Their first hit, the 1961 million-seller "Please Mr. Postman," was perhaps their biggest, a catchy lover's plea that would go down in history. It lived on the R&B charts for seven weeks at number 1, and was the first number 1 hit on the pop charts for the Motown label.

Janet Leigh in **Psycho**

MOViES OF THE
EARLY 1960s

The seeds of change that had taken root in the 1950s, such as the decline of the studio system and the breaking down of the "morality code," were ready to change the movie business forever. This was now the 1960s, where anything could happen and often did. Vibrant new actors and filmmakers were working alongside established stars, and many pushed the creative envelope, with good and bad results. The early years of the decade had a foot in both worlds, and that made it a very interesting time for moviegoers.

1961's "Best Picture" *West Side Story* did not capture the grit of rival street gangs as we would see it today, but its music (by Leonard Bernstein) and Romeo and Juliet story are timeless. As epics go, many people were more interested in the affair between co-stars Richard Burton

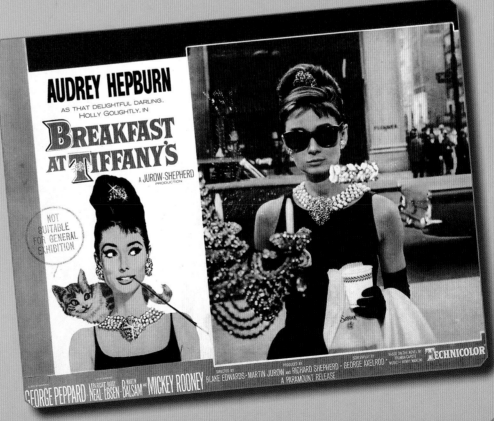

and Elizabeth Taylor than the film *Cleopatra,* but the sweeping majesty of *Lawrence of Arabia,* Best Picture winner of 1962, makes it one of the greatest films of this decade or any other.

More color barriers were broken in 1963 when Sidney Poitier became the first African American to win the "Best Actor" Oscar for *Lilies of the Field,* paving the way for many others to come.

This was also the time when director Alfred Hitchcock exchanged the suave Cary Grant of his 1950s movies for edgy Anthony Perkins in *Psycho,* which turned taking a shower into a nightmare for co-star Janet Leigh. Hitchcock also had something nasty to say about our feathered friends in *The Birds.* Meanwhile Audrey Hepburn captured our hearts in *Breakfast at Tiffany's,* Paul Newman hustled in *The Hustler* and *Hud,* Jack Lemmon and Lee Remick had one too many in *Days of Wine and Roses* and *The Magnificent Seven* rode into the sunset.

Peter O'Toole and Omar Sharif in **Lawrence of Arabia**

THE RONETTES

DJ Murray the K and The Ronettes

Unlike most girl groups of the era, this New York City trio found their niche as the street-savvy girls of poppy rock & roll. Their image included beehive hairdos, tight skirts, and dark makeup, and their big hits were "Be My Baby" and "Baby, I Love You." The group's greatest recordings were marked by "wall of sound" production, the signature of producer Phil Spector. Veronica "Ronnie" Bennett, the group's namesake, later married Spector, and then divorced him. In her biography *Be My Baby: How I Survived Mascara, Miniskirts, and Madness, or My Life as a Fabulous Ronette*, Ronnie reveals their strange past together, personally and professionally. I remember she told me he prevented her from performing any of the songs they recorded together.

Roy Orbison

There have been few artists more talented, or more gentle of spirit, than Roy Orbison. He brought a mix of rockabilly and country to rock & roll in a way no one had before, and graced every recording with his incredible, quivering vocals. No doubt he was a haunting balladeer, but he could just as easily jerk a tear from your eye as get you strutting to the burly beats of "Dream Baby" or "Oh, Pretty Woman," his signature song from 1964.

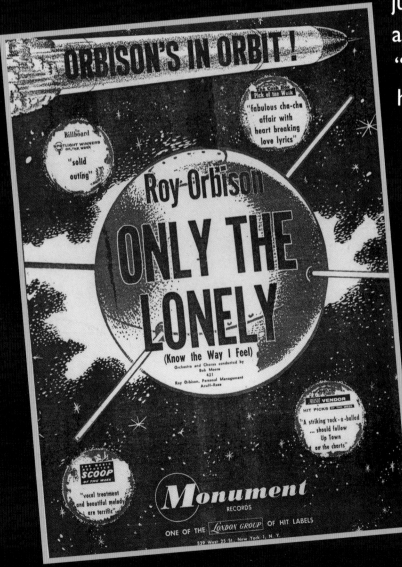

Favoring black clothes and donning dark shades to hide his chronic astigmatism, Orbison endured so much pain in his life. He lost his first wife when she fell from his motorcycle in 1966 (years before, Roy had written the song "Claudette" for her and gave it to the Everly Brothers; it was the B-side to "All I Have to Do Is Dream") and in 1968 he lost two of his three sons in a house fire. On the song "In Dreams," he's visited by a loved one in the night, only to find himself alone again in the morning.

was hurt by life, but he never
me as an angry man. He always
sweet and shy. I remember a
was hosting in New England,
Roy was scheduled to appear
de Johnny Rivers, Carl Perkins,
Brown, and Chuck Berry. We
standing together when Roy's

bus pulled up. He stepped ou
us all a friendly wave, and retur
the bus until showtime. Once o
though, he gave himself over
the crowd, and they gave hin
of love in return. After his fa
performance, Roy just got back
bus and disappeared.

The Kinks

Herman's Hermits

The Beatles

The Rolling Stones

CHAPTER 4

1964-1966

Attack of the Union Jack

When the first wave of British bands—the Beatles, the Dave Clark Five, the Animals—crashed on US shores, it was obvious to American artists that the new sound of rock & roll was based on their own homegrown music. From the blues-based guitar riffs to the wailing vocals, which never carried a whiff of English accent, every note that came across the Atlantic might as well have been stamped "Made in the USA."

But in the hands of the Brits, American music was completely re-energized. It was delivered with a punch that staggered listeners in a way the most aggressive mainstream musicians had not yet imagined possible. Think of the wall-shaking drums in the Dave Clark Five's "Glad All Over" or the raspy guitar crunch of the Kinks' "You Really Got Me." Listen to Eric Burdon's vocal howl in the Animals' "We Gotta Get Out of This Place." Rest assured, cousins, there was also great music by American players—but nothing with that energy or force.

Even the deep emotion of Motown, the good-time sounds of surf, and the liberating rhythms of rockabilly that sent kids running to the dance floor were overwhelmed by the powerful

introducing...
THE BEATLES
ENGLANDS No.1 VOCAL GROUP

VeeJay

The Beatles

Slay Shea Stadium

It was August 15, 1965 when the Beatles first performed at New York's Shea Stadium for the biggest rock & roll audience that had ever gathered in one place. Beatlemania was in full swing, and the band had booked a ten-city tour of stadiums. With more than 55,000 fans jamming the stadium in the borough of Queens, Shea was the crown jewel of the tour.

I was lucky enough to help emcee the show. I remember standing onstage and looking around the stadium at this sea of teenagers (with a few very patient parents peppered in here and there). The audience was wild with anticipation, and there was the most powerful feeling of electricity in the air.

Backstage, John, Paul, George, and Ringo were goofing around as they warmed up on their instruments. They had arrived at the stadium in an armored truck—each of the guys wore a Wells Fargo star on his stage suit, as if the security detail wouldn't know who they were! But there was good reason for all of the safety measures taken. There were no fans allowed on the field, but with a crowd that big and that hungry you had to be ready for a riot or at least a stampede. I remember the look on Ed Sullivan's face before we took the stage together. As the screaming reached an incredible pitch, he looked back at me with this mixture of disbelief and fear, and said, "Cousin Brucie, is this going to be dangerous?"

I nodded my head to him.

"What should we do?" he asked.

"Pray, Ed. Pray."

He looked at me with his eyes wide open, then turned and walked up the stage steps like a man headed to the gallows. Sullivan had always looked like he was starched and stiff—this time, he had good reason.

Talking to the Beatles before they performed, I could tell everyone was a little bit nervous. It wasn't just stage jitters, either—it was riot jitters. John, too, had asked me, "Coozin, is it safe?" and I remember reassuring him that everything was under control, even if I wasn't 100 percent sure of it myself. He also wanted to know that all of the fans were safe and being treated well. With a security crew of 2,000, I think it never got much worse than carrying all the girls who fainted into the hospital tents set up on the field. That and getting your ears blown out by all the screaming were about the biggest risks that night.

We finally announced the Beatles, and the fans absolutely lost their minds as the band took the stage at 9:17 pm and lit into "Twist and Shout." From the very start of their set, the band could barely be heard over the screaming crowd. Years later, George told *Musician* magazine that they "were not quite sure if anybody [could] even see us, let alone hear us." Despite rows of amplifiers and stage monitors, the band could hardly hear themselves play even though the closest spectators were clear across the baseball diamond from where the band was set up at second base. In the movie *The Beatles at Shea Stadium*, you can see them cracking up as John plays his Vox organ with his elbows on "I'm Down," the last song of their set. It was his response to the fact that nobody—including the band itself—could tell what was being played over the screaming crowd. Nonetheless, they played well (I think) and everybody had an incredibly good time.

The mainstream press had always been tough on the Beatles, and even on their fans. After the Shea show, the *New York Times* reported:

Several of the fans in the first row of the grandstands moaned, wept and called to the special police on the field: "Please, please. Give us some blades of the grass. They walked on the grass."

A passing policewoman observed: "They are psychos. Their mothers ought to see them now."

The unbelievable noise at Beatles shows represented how the phenomenon of Beatlemania had superceded the music. It bothered the group, too, and the next year they retired as touring musicians. Except for a couple of surprise shows and rooftop performances, the Beatles had left the building.

But seeing them in concert was only one way to grab a piece of the Beatles. Of course, the merchandise had been over the top: There were Beatles buttons, wigs, shirts, mugs, clocks, lunchboxes, charms, patches, posters, cups, neckties, ceramic statues, record players, watches, keyrings…somebody out there was probably selling Beatles underwear! Anyone who didn't catch them live still had a chance to see them in the movies. Though fans screamed in the theaters, too, the guys loomed larger than life in *Help!*, *A Hard Day's Night*, *Magical Mystery Tour*, and the psychedelic cartoon *Yellow Submarine*.

Once they gave up touring, the Beatles took their recording career to all new heights. But, boy, it sure was a kick to be in the same room—or even the same huge stadium—as the Fab Four.

In the hands of the Brits, American music was completely re-energized.

music of the British Invasion. UK artists had learned their trade by following in the footsteps of US musicians, but on arriving in America they became the leaders. It was their sound, and not America's own, that gave rock & roll a much-needed swift kick in the pants during the 1960s.

Remember that old grade-school history lesson about Paul Revere's midnight ride? Though we know now that his story was embellished in the name of patriotism, Revere is remembered for rousing half of Boston from bed with his famous warning: "The British are coming! The British are coming!" That's what it was like for the American bands of mid-1960s. The British Invasion was a wake-up call.

Taken to an Extreme

The past hundred years of music show that the listening public requires excess—something in the extreme—in order to change direction. Without it, we'd just mull along to the same sounds from yesteryear. We would all be sitting here in the twenty-first century humming along to "Paper Doll" from 1943. That was a great song, but I don't think the Mills Brothers would have gone over too well with a crowd dropping acid in a California commune. Extreme times call for extreme measures.

Huge changes to America's way of life were underfoot in the mid 1960s. So intense were the simmering social, political, racial, and sexual issues of the 1960s that musical artists could never have represented them in song alone. Instead, the full range of emotion came pouring out of them by every available means of expression. Not only were the songs infused with newfound intensity, but in live performances the musicians communicated with dramatic body

The Kinks

Sharp, witty, and sarcastic, the Kinks slashed through the British Invasion's pop moppets the way Dave Davies slashed the speakers on his Elpico guitar amp to achieve his distorted guitar tone on the band's hard-driving 1964 hit "You Really Got Me." Brother Ray Davies broke new ground lyrically with songs like "Dedicated Follower of Fashion," which lampooned the dandies of London's Carnaby Street. He raised the game for fellow lyricists like the Who's Pete Townshend, who has said Davies "invented a new kind of language for pop writing." In 1970, "Lola," Davies's hilarious-yet-touching tale of a confused encounter with a transvestite, became a huge hit in both the UK and the US—and, incidentally, was banned by many radio stations. Later that decade, Van Halen's raunchy cover of "You Really Got Me" and The Pretenders' tender "Stop Your Sobbing" proved what an important early influence the Kinks were on both heavy metal and punk/new wave.

The Mamas & the Papas

Blending two female with two male voices, this group took vocal harmony on a trip where it had never ventured before. Part folk, part pop, and all hippie, the Mamas and the Papas epitomized the romantic view of California as a sunny hippie haven with "California Dreamin'," their debut single. Among the hits to follow was their lush cover of the Shirelles' "Dedicated to the

One I Love." While their harmonies were produced with a much grander sound than the bare, minimalist approach of doo wop recordings, "Dedicated" has a spoken intro that is straight out of the doo wop tradition. The standout singer in the group was Cass Elliott, a sassy, full-figured gal whose huge pipes and even bigger charm made an unlikely hit of the group's cover of the 1930s jazz standard "Dream a Little Dream of Me." John Phillips, the group's leader, helped organize the Monterey International Pop Festival, which exposed legions of listeners to artists like Jimi Hendrix and Janis Joplin.

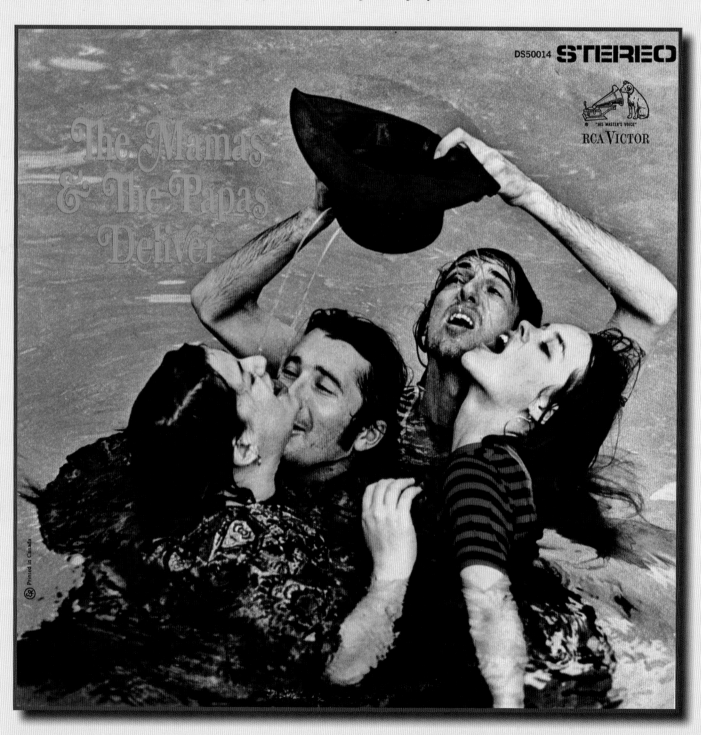

The Temptations

Signed to Motown in 1961, the quintet combined irresistible melodies and flawless harmonies with snappy choreography—achieving their biggest hits when Berry Gordy handed them to Smokey Robinson, who was writing and producing for Motown while pursuing his own career as a performer. With tenor Eddie Kendrick's sweet voice out front, Robinson crafted the Temptations' most enduring hits: "The Way You Do the Things You Do," "My Girl," "Since I Lost My Baby," and "Get Ready." In 1966, Norman Whitefield took over as the group's producer and brought baritone David Ruffin to the fore, giving the group a new toughness and their sixth number 1 R&B hit, "I Wish It Would Rain."

PETER & GORDON

This British Invasion duo recorded and performed a handful of songs written by Paul McCartney. McCartney was dating Peter Asher's sister, and the two were close friends. Peter and Gordon enjoyed years of success, recording big hits like "A World Without Love" and "Lady Godiva." Asher went on to become a hugely successful agent and producer.

language. Picture Mick Jagger with his hips thrown back, his arms outstretched, and his face in a grimace. As the Rolling Stones hammered out "(I Can't Get No) Satisfaction" behind him, Jagger's impossibly long fingers pointed into the crowd: *You—wake up!*

James Brown, too, would drench his three-piece suits as his body trembled and shook to "It's a Man's Man's Man's World." There was more than a little showmanship at work when James' manager took him from the stage draped in a blanket, but the message was that the world was too much for even the Godfather of Soul to bear.

Years before the Who, the Move, and Jimi Hendrix trashed their gear onstage, Paul Revere and the Raiders turned the concert stage into a circus ring. The band would throw themselves wildly across the platform, crashing into amplifiers and drum kits, until the finale when Paul lit a piano on fire. Fashion provided another vehicle for artistic expression, and the Raiders did their whole Ringling Bros. routine while dressed like a brigade of Minutemen soldiers. Performers of the day bedecked themselves in outsized get-ups and

Martha and the Vandellas

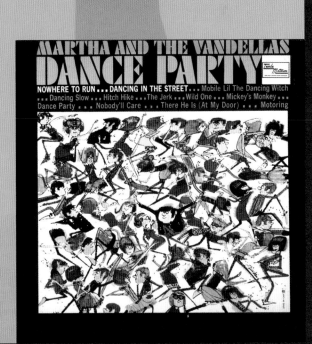

Martha Reeves and the Vandellas were a Motown trio combining the smooth sound of gospel with the hard edge of rhythm & blues. They recorded a string of chart toppers throughout the 1960s including their signature number, "Dancing in the Streets." Years later, Martha heard the call of public service and was elected councilwoman for the real "Motown"—that is, the city of Detroit, Michigan.

HOLY POP CULTURE!
IT'S BATMAN ON TV

Burt Ward and Adam West in **Batman**

T he live-action Batman who debuted on television in January of 1966 was a far cry from the dark and shadowy figure who first appeared in a May 1939 edition of *Detective Comics*. The eerie vigilante of the comics was recreated as a campy do-gooder, plotlines about murder and hatred were replaced with bungled bank jobs, and satanic criminals were recast as dunderheaded clowns.

But never was there anything quite as much fun to watch on TV.

Batman's appeal was escapism, pure and simple. It was a send-up of the original comic, of detective shows and spy movies, and of a society at risk of taking itself too seriously. Hilarious exchanges between Batman, played by Adam West, and his earnest sidekick Robin (Burt Ward) revealed that all was not entirely well between the bat ears of this hokey hero:

ROBIN: *Batman, maybe I should stay home tonight. Homework, you know.*

BATMAN: *I think you should acquire a taste for opera, Robin, as one does for poetry and olives.*

Though the show was all camp and eye candy, it really was innovative. Animated exclamations broke into the middle of live-action fight sequences—*Pow! Boof!*—and were synched to blasts from

action more fun to watch, but was also a subtle message that our lives aren't always so flat and simple. We get tilted and tossed around. Life doesn't happen parallel to the axis.

Even in this kitschy incarnation, *Batman* also was a reminder that we all have two sides: one that appears simple and good, one dark and perhaps flirting with evil. Neil Hefti's theme song,

the soundtrack's horn section. Usually those fights were taking place in the lair of a villain like the Joker, the Riddler, or the Penguin. Those bad-guy hideouts were never on an even plane; the sets were filmed as if the whole room was tilted by about 20 degrees. It made the

styled on Henry Mancini's theme for *Peter Gunn*, represented that perfectly. It got your attention, even made you a little nervous. That music was like the Bat Signal in the sky. It was a searchlight reflected on a cloud over Gotham, translated into music.

YARDBIRDS

In addition to producing six Top 40 singles, the Yardbirds introduced the world to three of the most influential guitarists in rock: Jimmy Page, Eric Clapton, and Jeff Beck. Beck played the unforgettable lead line on "Heart Full of Soul," which went to number 9 in 1965.

kaleidoscopic colors, with perhaps no one glittering more blindingly than the King, Elvis Presley. Meanwhile, people like the Four Seasons, Roy Orbison, and the delightful Petula Clark dressed in a more subdued manner even when their music was rocking & rolling.

If It's too Loud, You're too Old

The crackling energy of rock & roll could not be contained, and it came screaming out of the speakers of portable radios, car stereos, and turntables. Rock & roll itself was a primal scream; like no style before, it depended on volume. Love ballads had their place, and every band sang 'em, but to capture the right spirit, the music had to be played loud enough to boil your blood. Playing a rock tune back at paint-peeling volumes somehow aided the musical catharsis; if you couldn't shout at the top of your lungs, your favorite group was going to do it for you.

Of course, a huge fringe benefit was that when music was turned up, old folks were turned off. The willingness to be bludgeoned by volume was a bond among the brotherhood of rock &

The Rascals

Formed in New York, the Rascals broke onto the blue-eyed soul and rock scene with their cover of the Olympics' "Good Lovin'." The song hit number 1 and paved the way for the Rascals' release of their own material. When the group recorded "People Gotta Be Free," the record company was put off by the politicism and didn't want to be involved, but the group stuck to their guns—and the song went to number 1. Their hit single "Groovin'" still bounces around the airwaves today, and every time I hear it, I wish the Rascals would reunite.

The Supremes

The Supremes escaped the poverty of a Detroit housing project to become not only the best-selling *girl* group of the 1960s, but the best-selling African American group. The members of the Supremes—Diana Ross, Florence Ballard, and Mary Wilson—had been recruited by singer Paul Williams, while still in high school, to form the Primettes as a sister act to his popular Detroit group, the Primes (who later became the Temptations). The girls showed up regularly at Motown's "Hitsville" office after school until Berry Gordy agreed to sign them in 1961—though Gordy, being something of a father figure to the artists on his label, wouldn't sign them until they finished

high school. Gordy shifted Diana Ross to lead vocals and assigned them to the in-house writing and production team of Brian Holland, Lamont Dozier, and Eddie Holland. Holland/Dozier/Holland gave the girls their first number 1 hit with "Where Did Our Love Go" in 1964. At a time when racial divides were crumbling, Gordy made sure the Supremes appealed—with a polished sound and a sophisticated look—to both black and white audiences. The Supremes struck gold with their elegant soul, garnering twelve number 1 hits between 1964 and 1969, including a record-breaking streak of five consecutive number 1's in 1965. A string of classics followed, many penned by Holland/Dozier/Holland, including "Baby Love," "Stop! In the Name of Love," and "I Hear a Symphony."

DUSTY SPRINGFIELD

At the beginning of the British Invasion, American and UK artists were cross-pollinating their audiences, carrying the seeds of soul and rock & roll back and forth across the ocean. Dusty Springfield was immeasurably responsible for introducing the sound of rhythm & blues to the Brits—and sending it back stateside with such passion and purity that she was referred to for a time as the "White Negress." Adjusting for political correctness, she's gone down in history as the queen of white soul. Dusty first knocked our socks off in 1963 with "I Only Want to Be with You" and followed with hits including "Wishin' & Hopin'," "You Don't Have to Say You Love Me" (an English-language version of the Italian hit "Io Che Non Vivo (Senzate)"), and Burt Bacharach's "The Look of Love." We lost Dusty in 1999 to breast cancer, and I'll always miss her.

MANFRED MANN

Part of the wave of British blues-influenced bands that included the Stones and the Yardbirds, Manfred Mann struck gold in 1964 with the rockin' "Do Wah Diddy Diddy." The song had been a minor hit in '63 for a female-led American group called the Exciters.

rollers, and it helped establish a closed circle of proud (albeit going deaf) young listeners and players who excluded anyone too old or too meek.

Despite the wishes of moms and dads everywhere, rock & roll just wouldn't go quietly. Volume was part and parcel of the new "heaviness" in rock. It sounded loud even when the dial was set low because the songs were thickly painted with dissonance and, sometimes, planned distortion. Rock took several cues from blues music, including the use of tense chord changes; the discordant sounds were the sonic equivalent of sand in Vaseline. Ear-bending harmonies were hammered home on guitars that sounded like they'd been put through a blender.

Why has the electric guitar always been rock & roll's instrument of choice? I think it's because the guitar is such a personal instrument. Unlike a piano or a bass fiddle, the guitar is played like it's connected to your body. There's this electric current flowing from your heart to your fingers and across the neck of a guitar. You caress the strings, you bend them, you make them cry. And you send all of your internal emotion

1965 GT Fastback

The Ford Mustang

Like the untamable animal that gave the car its name, the Ford Mustang was a beautiful beast. Debuting in 1964, the Mustang defined the "pony car" class and was ideally suited to a personal style. Not nearly as wide as Mom and Dad's clunker, the 'Stang was never too much or too little car; you could take three friends with you to the drive-in, or cruise the streets solo without being surrounded by too much metal and leather. In fact, the only way to make the Mustang appear any cooler than it already did was to have a great-looking companion riding shotgun.

With a front end that looked like it was itching for a fight and a motor that sounded like an electric guitar, the Mustang realized Ford's dream of selling a youthful auto that would seat four in bucket seats, have a floor-mounted shifter, and sell for under $2,500. And sell it did! Following an aggressive ad campaign, Ford moved 22,000 Mustangs on the car's first day in the showroom, and within four months had sold 100,000. In music terms, that's a gold record.

The Civil Rights Act of 1964

President Kennedy first asked for legislation "giving all Americans the right to be served in facilities which are open to the public" in his famous civil rights address to the nation in 1963. The bill he introduced to Congress outlawed the Jim Crow laws that had dictated "separate but equal" segregation of blacks from whites, and was strengthened to prohibit workplace discrimination against both African Americans and women. This landmark act made discrimination based on race—and gender—illegal. After a tough fight in Congress, the bill was signed into law by President Johnson on July 2, 1964. Sadly, President Kennedy didn't live to see the law passed.

The Troggs

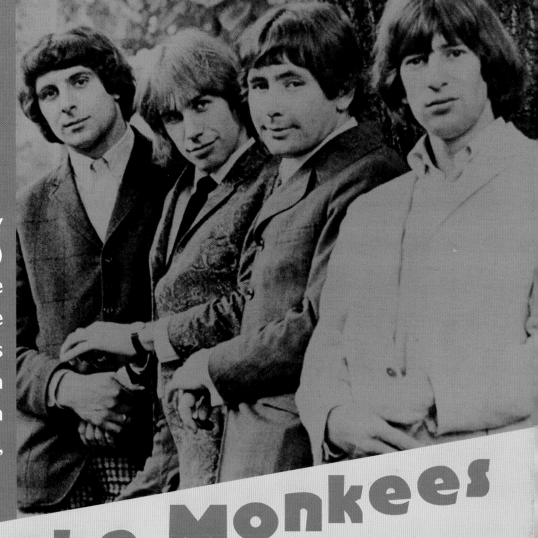

The Troggs (originally called the Troglodytes) defined the garage rock sound with raw, simple rockers like their most famous hit, "Wild Thing." The British band was a huge influence on punks like the Stooges, MC5, and the Ramones.

The Monkees

Mop-topped and cute as...well, cute as four chimps playing music, the Monkees were invented by two television executives who wanted to recreate Beatles-styled zaniness for the small screen. Had musical talent been a factor, perhaps some who auditioned for the band—like Stephen Stills and Harry Nilsson—would have gotten the gig. Still, the Monkees scored memorable sugar-pop hits with "Last Train to Clarksville," "Pleasant Valley Sunday," and Neil Diamond's "I'm a Believer."

Columbia
Stereo
KG 31120

BOB
DYLAN'S
GREATEST
HITS
VOL.II

BOB DYLAN

The social revolutionaries of the 1960s were not armed with weapons: They were armed with acoustic guitars and deeply questioning lyrics. The commander in chief of the peace movement in music was Bob Dylan, a prolific singer/songwriter whose countercultural themes tackled Vietnam, civil rights, drug culture, and nuclear apocalypse—not to mention countless odes to peace and love. The tireless theme of change infused many of his greatest hits, including "Blowin' in the Wind," "The Times They Are a-Changin'," "A Hard Rain's a-Gonna Fall," "Like a Rolling Stone," and "Subterranean Homesick Blues."

Dylan may not have asked for the kingly praise heaped upon him, but he's always been regarded as a visionary hell-bent on changing the world. He even altered his own persona and musical personality, and ruffled the feathers of his folkie fan base by plugging in an electric guitar at the Newport Folk Festival in 1965. His profound influence on fellow musicians—from John Lennon and Jimi Hendrix to Joni Mitchell, Mick Jagger, and Bruce Springsteen—is hard to overestimate.

TOM JONES

If tight pants, open shirts, and a throaty baritone—plus legions of swooning ladies—don't spell rock & roll, what does? Tom Jones was a bonafide member of the British Invasion, and got his start singing for a beat band in his native South Wales. He first hit with "It's Not Unusual" in 1965, following by radio staples like "What's New Pussycat," "Delilah," and "Green Green Grass of Home," inspired by a version he'd heard by Jerry Lee Lewis. To this day, Tom can't get through a tune onstage without faint female fans tossing him their undergarments. Poor Tom.

straight through a cable and out to an amplifier so it can be broadcast across the rooftops. For a long time, the guitar had been symbolic of frontier life out in the wild west—probably best represented by Gene Autry, the Singing Cowboy. But Autry played an acoustic guitar. Once the thing was plugged in, all bets were off.

It's interesting, too, that the electric guitar would be so popular among young players when its key developers hailed from the previous generation. Their names, emblazoned on the most widely used guitar gear available, became synonymous with rock & roll: Les Paul and Leo Fender created the prototypes from which all electric guitars would be built, and a vast number of players plugged those six-strings into a wall of amplifiers designed by a British music store owner named Jim Marshall.

Distorted guitars played off of the drums, their primal rhythmic counterpart, and conspired with weighty bass guitar parts to rattle your spine. Plus, the new crop of '60s heroes looked a heck of a lot cooler with an electric guitar hanging around their neck. To this day, the electric guitar—preferably, one played

The Hollies

This well-loved British pop group mixed vocal harmonies with their singular skill in crafting pop songs. They had a slew of hit singles in the 1960s, including "Bus Stop" and "Carrie Anne." In 1970, the Hollies recorded the powerful ballad "He Ain't Heavy, He's My Brother," which was read both as a civil rights song and a Vietnam song.

The Fortunes

"You've Got Your Troubles" introduced the bouncy, harmony-driven sound of British invaders the Fortunes to the world when it cracked both the US and British Top 10 in 1965. The Fortunes were also the voices of Coca-Cola, singing the 1969 jingle "It's the Real Thing."

ABOVE: *Patrick Macnee and Diana Rigg are The Avengers.*
INSET: *Patrick McGoohan as "Secret Agent Man."*
OPPOSITE PAGE: *David McCallum, Robert Vaughn, and Leo G. Carroll in The Man from U.N.C.L.E.*

SPY TV

By the mid 1960s, we were crazy for spy stories, and television was the perfect medium for it. *The Man from U.N.C.L.E.* was prime time's answer to James Bond. With Robert Vaughn as Napoleon Solo and David McCallum as Illya Kuryakin battling the evil THRUSH, it was a runaway hit. *I Spy* debuted shortly after *U.N.C.L.E.*, featuring two government spies who were a bit more down to earth than James Bond–style superheroes. The show starred Robert Culp, but is best known for introducing television audiences to the first African American man in a leading role, co-star Bill Cosby.

In 1966 the British invasion was in full swing, and that invasion included one of the best male/female teams in television history, *The Avengers*, starring Patrick Macnee as dapper John Steed and Diana Rigg as the smart and sexy Emma Peel. The show had been a favorite in the UK for years, with Honor Blackman teaming with the impeccable Macnee. She left the series and went on the prowl as Pussy Galore in *Goldfinger*, paving the way for Diana Rigg's entrance as Mrs. Peel.

We all know Johnny Rivers' 1966 song "Secret Agent Man", particularly since it keeps showing up in pop culture venues. But, it was used as a theme song for another British spy import: *Secret Agent* starring Patrick McGoohan. Called *Danger Man* in the UK, the show featured secret agent John Drake—a man who depended more on his wits than firepower. Later in the decade, McGoohan co-created and starred in the television cult classic *The Prisoner,* about a former rebellious spy who is held captive in a surreal and deadly village.

Bill Cosby and Robert Culp in I Spy

FRANK ZAPPA AND THE MOTHERS OF INVENTION

Frank Zappa (bottom right)

His music, lyrics, and album covers might lead you to believe that he was just a wild guy out for laughs, but Frank Zappa had one of the finest creative minds in the business. Zappa's unique brand of mania was informed by his deep understanding of contemporary classical music, oddly coupled with an affinity for doo wop. With and without the Mothers of Invention, Zappa and his sidemen slipped exquisite musicianship between satirical lyrics on late-'60s albums like *Freak Out!*, *We're Only in it for the Money*, and *Burnt Weeny Sandwich*.

Sonny & Cher

In the early days they were known as Caesar and Cleo, and occasionally provided backup vocals on Phil Spector recordings. The husband and wife duo became an overnight sensation with the success of their single "I Got You Babe." The number 1 song led to several other hits and the duo eventually got their own variety show: *The Sonny & Cher Comedy Hour.*

through an amplifier "turned to 11"—is an enduring symbol of rock & roll.

What Was That You Said?

Volumes upon volumes of books have been dedicated to the lyrics of '60s rock artists. The words of our heroes continue to be documented, analyzed, and dissected in what amounts to pop culture's longest-running science experiment. Chances are good that you can belt out your favorite '60s hits in your head without even glancing at the liner notes. Still, a lot of people get so carried away by the music that they don't always catch the meaning of the words as they sing along.

In songs of the '60s, the weight of the music was being matched pound for pound with lyrics that were increasingly dark and questioning. Tales of love won and love lost will always be favorite subjects for songwriters, but once the British Invasion bands started pushing the envelope on rock's instrumental sound, artists also started exploring lyrical themes with more heaviness. So, at the same time Bobby Hebb was holding up the bright side of the charts with "Sunny," the Rolling Stones

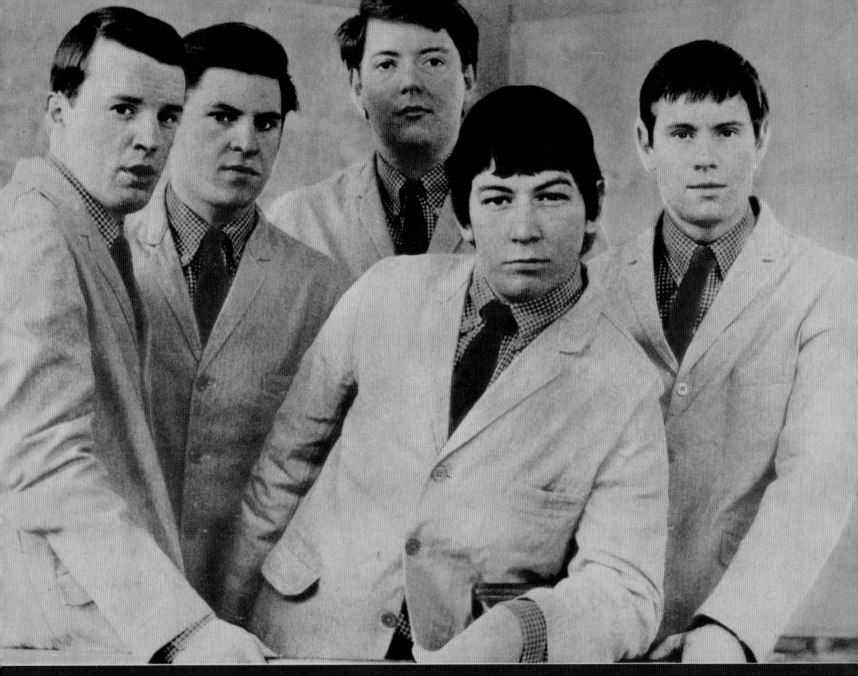

Eric Burdon
and the Animals

Drawing heavily on the blues, Eric Burdon and the Animals brought true grit to the early British Invasion. Burdon's powerful voice ripped through classics like "The House of the Rising Sun" and "We Gotta Get Out of This Place," giving pop a new, hard rock edge.

were taking darker turns on "Paint It Black."

The Stones were never a band to sing a simple song, and they didn't want their listeners to oversimplify their own lives, either. In "Nineteenth Nervous Breakdown" Mick Jagger tells a spoiled girl, whose mother had neglected her, that she "better stop, look around" before she's swallowed up by her own misery. The Standells, a gritty Los Angeles band, offered up a big bad story in their 1965 hit, "Dirty Water" (still played at Boston's Fenway Park after every Red Sox victory); if you read between the lines, it appears that the first-person storyteller just might be the Boston Strangler. And in "Season of the Witch," Donovan similarly portrays an era of suspicion and mistrust:

When I look over my shoulder,
what do you think I see?

Some other cat looking
over his shoulder at me

No Jokes from the Folks

Purist folk musicians of the 1960s sidestepped the volume and dissonance of rock, relying instead on the time-honored pairing of an acoustic guitar with unadorned vocals. But just because they could sing the songs around a campfire didn't mean their message was any less intense.

In fact, folk singers were explicit with their anti-establishment views and expressed them in lengthy tunes that browbeat the government, demanded change, and railed against convention. That's always been a role of folk singers from the ancient days of the minstrels: to share the experience of the common man in his ongoing struggle against the powers that be. Folk singers are the bell ringers of their time.

Folk had recently enjoyed a revival in the 1950s, with players like Pete Seeger and Woody Guthrie at the vanguard. Though their methods of resistance were inherently passive—after all, they were only strumming guitars and singing— both of them were pretty gutsy. Woody Guthrie had a handmade sticker on his acoustic guitar that read THIS MACHINE KILLS FASCISTS, and when Senator Joe McCarthy and friends went hunting for Red sympathizers in the 1950s, Seeger was put on a blacklist. For Seeger, it was a clear-cut moral issue: no one should

Petula Clark

This charismatic British pop singer found enormous international success with her upbeat sound and universal appeal. Her most famous cut, "Downtown," was inspired by a visit to New York City and was a best seller in English, French, Italian, and German translations. Pet was recently my guest on a rock & roll show on PBS television, where she continued to turn on her amazing charm and undeniable talent. She continues to record—and occasionally puts pen to paper on behalf of an old friend (see our Preface, page 10). I'm just crazy about her.

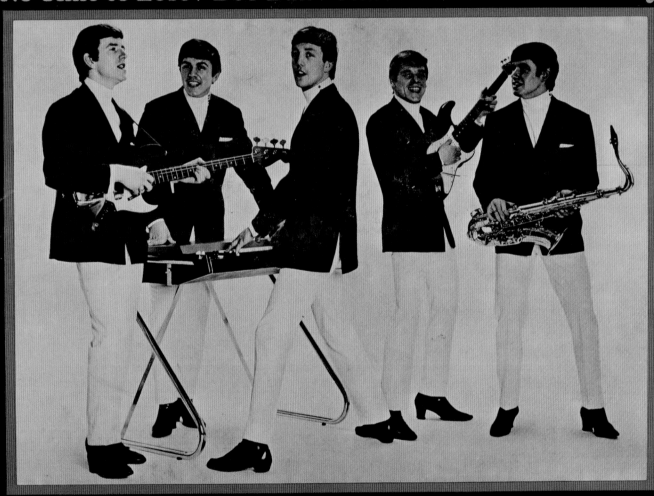

DAVE CLARK FIVE

In the early days of the British Invasion, the two bands that made the girls scream the most were the Beatles and the Dave Clark Five. Although the Liverpool foursome edged out the five Londoners, no other British band came near the Dave Clark Five's feat of placing fifteen consecutive singles in the US Top 40 from 1964 to 1966. The band sold fifty million records with catchy dance numbers like "Glad All Over" and "Bits and Pieces." The DC5 appeared on the Ed Sullivan show eighteen times; the Beatles, only four times.

TOTAL KNOCKOUT

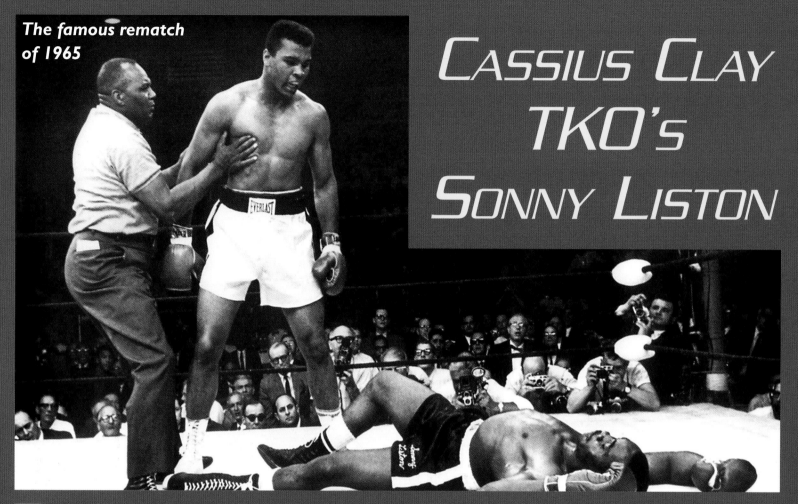

The famous rematch of 1965

CASSIUS CLAY TKO's SONNY LISTON

Bookies had put the odds at seven to one against a young Cassius Clay when he was scheduled to fight heavyweight champ Charles "Sonny" Liston at Miami Beach in February of 1964. After all, Clay may have been an Olympic Gold boxer but nobody thought this rhyming, jaw-flappin' pretty boy could take the feared and revered Liston, who was a tough ex-con. But Clay unleashed such a storm in Round 6 that Liston refused to leave his corner at the start of Round 7.

The next day, the new heavyweight champ changed to his name to Cassius X (like other members of the Nation of Islam, such as Malcom X, Cassius jettisoned his last name, believing it was the legacy of slave culture) and it wasn't long before he changed it again. Muhammad Ali would become known throughout the world as one of the finest athletes in history.

A year after the fight, Ali and Liston fought a rematch on May 25, 1965, which Ali won in a first-round KO.

have to sign a document saying they were or were not a communist. Not in his beloved America.

The revival carried into the '60s, and by the middle of the decade folkies had plenty to sing about. Folk singers' cries against the Vietnam War, in particular, helped fuel a movement that would soon become more vocal and more violent. Among the many anti-war folk songs (see *Anti-War Songs* on page 241) was "Eve of Destruction" sung by Oklahoma's Barry McGuire. With challenging lyrics, the song likened the bloody fighting in the Far East to the harsh racial divisions here at home:

> *Think of all the hate there*
> *is in Red China*
> *Then take a look around*
> *to Selma, Alabama*

Another of the many examples was "Where Have All the Flowers Gone?" Joan Baez, Peter, Paul & Mary, and the Kingston Trio all had hits with Pete Seeger's tune, which told in melancholy verses how all of our young men had been turned into soldiers, and all the soldiers turned toward the grave.

Rock & roll was folk's younger sibling,

Donovan

This Scottish folk rocker—often referred to as the Scottish Bob Dylan—released the first-ever rock box set with his dual album *A Gift from a Flower to a Garden*. His psychedelic hits included the groovy "Mellow Yellow" and the bouncy "There is a Mountain."

THE ROLLING STONES

The longest-running—and many say the greatest—rock band in history, the Rolling Stones have rolled through four decades without deviating from their blues-based, guitar-driven sound. The Stones broke through in 1964 with a raucous cover of Bobby Womack's "It's All Over Now." The band found its own powerful voice in 1965 with the hit singles "Last Time" and "(I Can't Get No) Satisfaction" and redefined rock & roll as a dangerous, anti-social force. As the counterculture became more militantly anti-establishment, the writing team of lead singer Mick Jagger and guitarist Keith Richards gave voice to its seething frustration and growing power as a force for change with songs like "Sympathy for the Devil" and "Street Fighting Man." The Stones led

the sexual revolution forward as well, with the blatant "Let's Spend the Night Together" and Mick Jagger's hyperactive charisma, occasionally swaying toward the romantic with songs like "She's a Rainbow" (a personal favorite). In 1971 the Stones kicked off their own record label with the sexy album *Sticky Fingers*, which yielded the racy tribute to interracial romance "Brown Sugar."

Great albums like *Goat's Head Soup* and *Some Girls* followed, proving the Stones could deliver heart-wrenching ballads ("Angie") and play with musical trends without losing their grit. Despite occasional estrangements between Jagger and Richards, the Glimmer Twins are still going strong—writing and recording great rock albums and touring the world in their sixties.

Raquel Welch in
One Million Years B.C.

Boom-Boom Goes the Bombshell

The 1960s exploded with vivid imagery, and in an era full of eye candy, few visions were sweeter to young men everywhere than the knock-'em-dead bombshells seen in movies and magazines. An increasingly permissive view on sex, too, helped fire the imagination in the age of swinging singles, short skirts, and long libidos.

Among the gorgeous women to walk off the silver screen and into the fantasies of overheated males was Julie Christie. A bright-eyed British beauty with talent to match her looks, Christie took the Oscar for Best Actress as Diana Scott in *Darling* (1965), fixing into the minds of boys everywhere that models really do sleep their way to success. The same year found her playing Lara Antipova in *Doctor Zhivago*.

As international doors swung open, few imports were more welcome than the lovely ladies from afar. Swiss actress Ursula Andress starred in the classic James Bond movie *Dr. No* (1962). Italian star Sophia Loren, a woman of incomparable beauty and class, stopped even the hearts of her co-stars, leaving the likes of Cary Grant, Frank Sinatra, and Peter Sellers completely smitten.

Raquel Welch was a top contender for the consummate American sex symbol. In a promotional poster for *One Million Years B.C.* (1966), Welch appeared in a prehistoric bikini (cavemen totally dug those things). Her poster far outsold the movie. Sinful thoughts about Welch were affirmed when she played the part of Lust, the seventh deadly sin, in *Bedazzled* (1967).

The Byrds

The bright, jangly guitars and complex vocal harmonies of the Byrds led the folk-rock movement onto the charts, of Bob Dylan's "Mr. Tambourine Man" in 1965. The gentle "Turn! Turn! Turn!" was another huge hit, with Pete Seeger's original lyrics

Folk singers were explicit with their anti-establishment views.

and their lyrical themes frequently ran parallel throughout the 1960s. But the feisty little brother would overtake his elder later in the decade and effectively put an end to folk's revival. Rather than fade out, a handful of folk artists crossed over to rock. If any single moment captured that shift, it was when Bob Dylan plugged in an electric guitar at the Newport Folk Festival in 1965. After performing on acoustic the night before, Dylan took the stage with a full-blown electric band (including Mike Bloomfield from the Paul Butterfield Blues Band on guitar and Al Kooper, later of Blood, Sweat & Tears fame, on keyboards) and lit into his new song "Maggie's Farm." The crowd full of folkies booed him off the stage. Dylan, considered by many to be the voice of his generation, had a tough time recovering that night, but in that bold moment he really opened the door for a new genre of music. Folk rock crossovers including Donovan, Buffalo Springfield, the Lovin' Spoonful, and the Byrds have Bob Dylan's electric guitar to thank for their long-running success. In case you haven't heard, Bob's career recovered, too.

Sleeping with the Enemy

The fact that rock & roll artists were selling a lot of records—and I mean *a lot* of records—brings us back around to an inconvenient reality for the anti-establishment, anti-capitalist crowd: The rising youth movement was one and the same with the rising youth market. The two were a yin-yang phenomenon, each feeding off the energy of the other. Not only record companies but Hollywood filmmakers, fashion designers, electronics companies, broadcasters, magazine publishers, and advertising agencies turned huge profits on a generation that defined itself in opposition to the big bad "money machine." The corporate world was selling back to young people their own rebellious culture.

Another way of saying it? The estab-

THE TURTLES

Merry folk rockers the Turtles followed the template set by the Byrds, breaking through by prettying up the Bob Dylan song "It Ain't Me, Babe," which reached the Top 10 in 1965. Their signature song, "Happy Together," went to number 1 in the summer of '67.

lishment was arming the resistance. That's a tough morsel to gnaw on, and even today the diehard rebels of the '60s probably won't swallow it too easily.

Tempting as it is to demonize authority, there was no evil plot at work. It was simple supply and demand. The young poets were free to be creative in their own circles—but were they going to manufacture vinyl records and establish distribution networks nationwide? No, they'd need the powers of industry for that. No one was going to build a radio tower out of flowers and gossamer.

For their own part, record companies of the 1960s were learning to capitalize on a market that was listening to music ever more carefully. The music-buying public was starting to look like a huge crowd of audiophiles, and if the labels were going to turn a dime they'd have to cater to their customers with higher fidelity recordings. The muddy live recordings of prior decades, made by bands who would set up their gear in an echo-filled room as if playing a live concert, were not going to cut it anymore. Inside the recording studios, veteran producers would need to start following the lead of creative young

Writer Truman Capote, second from right, and actress Lauren Bacall, far left, at a book party for In Cold Blood, *1966*

Books that Passed the Acid Test

Books in the 1960s were just as provocative as the clothes and music of the era. Jacqueline Susann's racy roman à clef *Valley of the Dolls*, with its tales of pill-popping beauties ("dolls" were downers), was a best seller. So was Truman Capote's *In Cold Blood*, his "nonfiction novel" about the murder of a Kansas wheat farmer and his family by two ex-cons. Capote's book broke with journalistic convention by probing the psychology of the killers—turning a true crime story into great literature. The movie was a sensation as well. Capote set the stage for the New Journalism movement, which put aside "objective" reporting for colorful insider accounts like Tom Wolfe's *Electric Kool-Aid Acid Test* and Hunter S. Thompson's *Hell's Angels: The Strange and Terrible Saga of the Outlaw Motorcycle Gangs*.

Herman's Hermits

Following the success of their number 1 UK single "I'm Into Something Good," this Manchester pop band crossed the pond and swept the nation. They emphasized their English sound, riding the wave of the British Invasion and landing eight Top 10 singles in a span of two years—thanks to the mentoring of Peter Noone by a fellow named John Lennon.

The drug culture got a boost in 1965 when Harvard psychology professor Timothy Leary returned from Mexico, where he'd taken hallucinogenic mushrooms. Due to his own mind-expanding experiences, Leary believed psychedelics were therapeutic. He and his colleagues took prisoners on mushroom trips in an effort to change their criminal nature, and gave LSD to some 300 professors, grad students, writers, and philosophers. The attention their research received led to a black market for acid, which became illegal in 1966. An obsession of FBI agent G. Gordon Liddy, Leary was arrested for marijuana possession but escaped to Switzerland, which refused to extradite him. Labeled "the most dangerous man in America" by President Nixon (the *actual* most dangerous man in America), he was captured in 1973 and sentenced to ninety-five years in prison. California governor Jerry Brown released him in 1976. Leary went on his final trip on May 31, 1996. Friends at his bedside said Leary's final words were "Why not?"

Timothy Leary, circa 1965, from the documentary Timothy Leary's Dead

THE MOODY BLUES

An English band from Birmingham, the Moody Blues paved the way for progressive rock by combining pulsating rhythms, symphonic arrangements, synthesized sounds, and psychedelic lyrics. Their biggest hit was the eerie ballad "Nights in White Satin."

The Association

This California vocal band was a staple of AM radio in the late '60s and early '70s. Their tight, polished harmonies brought commercial success with singles like "Along Comes Mary" and "Cherish." The Association opened the legendary 1967 Monterey Pop Festival.

Paul Revere & the Raiders

"Indian Reservation" and the anti-drug song "Kicks" were just two of this Oregon rock group's biggest hits. Prone to some wild stage antics, they appeared multiple times on Dick Clark's *Where the Action Is*, assuming the role of America's response to the British Invasion.

musicians and audio engineers who saw untapped potential among the old recording technology and techniques.

In 1966, the Beach Boys released *Pet Sounds*, without a doubt one of the most ambitious and influential recordings of all time. The collection yielded a slew of big hits for the Boys, including "Wouldn't It Be Nice," "Sloop John B," the lush "God Only Knows," and "Caroline No." These were mainstream hits, for sure, but leader Brian Wilson's vision was as far from conventional as you could get. Mingling between the Beach Boys' well-combed vocal harmonies were unexpected blurbs from bicycle bells, barking dogs, and soda pop bottles. Though the original release was a monaural recording—it wasn't even stereo!—Wilson painstakingly built the recording with dozens of sounds layered one on top of the next. He created a pop symphony. In fact, the roster of musicians used on *Pet Sounds* was about twice the size of an orchestra: Added to the Beach Boys themselves were more than fifty session players lending their talent to parts for violin, accordion, ukelele, French horn, harmonica, saxophone,

The Four Tops

Led by Levi Stubbs' rough-hewn baritone, the Four Tops brought a tougher, more mature sound to Motown Records with powerful soul classics like the 1966 number 1 hit "Reach Out I'll Be There." The Tops began singing together in high school on Detroit's North End. Old friends with Motown founder Berry Gordy, they found a home at his label and were launched with the Holland/Dozier/Holland tune "Baby, I Need Your Loving," which went to number 11 in 1964. Fun fact: Levi Stubbs was the voice of the man-eating plant in *The Little Shop of Horrors* movie. FEED ME, Seymour!

Movie Musicals and Epics

For better or worse, sweeping epics and big-budget, family-friendly musicals were still Hollywood staples in the mid 1960s. Julie Andrews scored two big hits during this time with *Mary Poppins* and *The Sound of Music*. She played the role of Eliza Doolittle, the cockney flower girl transformed by Rex Harrison's Henry Higgins in the Broadway production of *My Fair Lady*, but the screen role went to Audrey Hepburn, who was the star of the moment when the movie was cast. Julie Andrews ended up winning the Oscar for *Mary Poppins* and the rest is history. *Oliver!*, based on Charles Dickens' *Oliver Twist,* and *Camelot*, starring Richard Harris as King Arthur and Vanessa Redgrave as Guenevere, came later in the decade.

No matter what your musical taste, the scores of all these movies had some

A LOVE CAUGHT IN THE FIRE OF REVOLUTION

Turbulent were the times and fiery was the love story of Zhivago, his wife... and the passionate, tender Lara.

METRO-GOLDWYN-MAYER presents A CARLO PONTI PRODUCTION

DAVID LEAN'S FILM OF BORIS PASTERNAK'S
DOCTOR ZHIVAGO

WINNER OF 6 ACADEMY AWARDS!

STARRING GERALDINE CHAPLIN · JULIE CHRISTIE · TOM COURTENAY
ALEC GUINNESS · SIOBHAN McKENNA · RALPH RICHARDSON
OMAR SHARIF (AS ZHIVAGO) · ROD STEIGER · RITA TUSHINGHAM
SCREEN PLAY BY ROBERT BOLT · DIRECTED BY DAVID LEAN · MUSIC BY MAURICE JARRE · IN PANAVISION® AND METROCOLOR MGM

Julie Andrews and Christopher Plummer (center) in **The Sound of Music**

really memorable songs: "Do-Re-Mi" and "My Favorite Things" from *The Sound of Music*; "Chim-Chim-Cheree" and "Let's Go Fly a Kite" from *Mary Poppins*; "With a Little Bit of Luck" and "Get Me to the Church on Time" from *My Fair Lady*; "Consider Yourself" from *Oliver!* and "If Ever I Would Leave You" from *Camelot*.

Director David Lean really knew his way around an epic, and he followed the success of *Lawrence of Arabia* with *Dr. Zhivago*, starring Omar Sharif as Zhivago, and the gorgeous Julie Christie as his great love, Lara. I think most men would have braved the brutal Russian winter to keep Lara warm. *A Man for all Seasons,* starring Paul Scofield as Sir Thomas More in his deadly struggle with England's King Henry VIII, played with gusto by Robert Shaw, is a low-key masterpiece which still resonates today.

Robert Shaw and Paul Scofield in **A Man for all Seasons**

Charlton Heston was the go-to guy for historical epics, playing Spanish hero Rodrigo Diaz in *El Cid,* teamed with the luscious Sophia Loren; British hero General Charles George "Chinese" Gordon in *Khartoum*; and Michelangelo in *The Agony and the Ecstasy.* However, these sorts of spectacles were soon to wind down as the decade started dealing in the present. During this time, audiences could also see Stanley Kubrick's doomsday opus, *Dr. Strangelove or: How I Learned to Stop Worrying and Love the Bomb* starring Peter Sellers and George C. Scott, Michael Caine's rakish lad in *Alfie,* Liz and Dick's boozing battles in *Who's Afraid of Virginia Woolf,* and David Hemmings' "Swinging London" photographer stepping in and out of reality with Vanessa Redgrave in *Blow Up.* Yes, the times they were a changin'.

MOD FASHIONS

Twiggy at a photo shoot, from the television special Twiggy: Why?

Mod fashion was bright, sexy, and streamlined: micro minis, shiny vinyl go-go boots, and swooping black eyeliner for women; tight suit coats, narrow lapels, and super-slim trousers for men. Born on London's hip Carnaby Street, mod was a reaction to the baggy, scruffy look of 1950s beatniks. The sharp, cool clothes and paintbox makeup from "London look" designers like Mary Quant and Biba were popularized in the United States by English dolly birds like mega-model Twiggy and Mick Jagger's girlfriend Chrissy Shrimpton. British bands like the Who, the Kinks, and Small Faces took mod style around the world.

Lovin' Spoonful

A fixture on the Top 40 charts in the mid '60s, the Lovin' Spoonful found great success by mixing folk-rock roots with sweet pop, as heard on the hit "Do You Believe in Magic?"

Gerry & the Pacemakers

Based in Liverpool and managed by Brian Epstein, this British sensation was one of the Beatles' earliest rival. They had huge UK hits in "Ferry Cross the Mersey," "How Do You Do It," "I Like It," and "I'll Be There." Their clean-cut image and catchy pop captured imaginations in the US as well. Lead vocalist Gerry Marsden is a natural onstage and the Brits have always loved him.

A huge fringe benefit was that when music was turned up, old folks were turned off.

and more. Utilizing overdubbing or "sound on sound" recording (a technique pioneered by Les Paul in 1950, which allowed performances to be independently created and then added to the whole), no single pet sound went to tape until it passed first through Wilson's critical ear.

More notable than the song compositions themselves, Brian Wilson's production approach to *Pet Sounds* reinvented the recording studio as a new instrument. Artists from Eric Clapton to Bob Dylan to Elton John have sung the album's praises, and you can hear in their own productions how carefully their ears were tuned to *Pet Sounds*. It's been hailed by music critics as one of the greatest recordings ever made, often falling second only to the album it so deeply influenced: the Beatles' *Sgt. Pepper's Lonely Hearts Club Band*. Paul McCartney, as well as

producer George Martin and others, has said that without *Pet* there would have been no *Pepper*.

Amped for a Fight

All of these new extremes in music—the feverish performances, the amped-up volume, the dissonant undertones, the elaborate recordings—were part of youth's refusal to be complacent. We were painting with a hundred new colors, and every one of them looked good on the canvas. On the charts, Patti Page was neighbors with Petula Clark, Gary Lewis and the Playboys lived with the Beach Boys, and the Yardbirds coexisted with the Turtles.

The British Invasion artists had pushed us to think harder and play harder. In the days to come, youth culture would put its new armor to the test as the revolution in music became part of a very real rebellion.

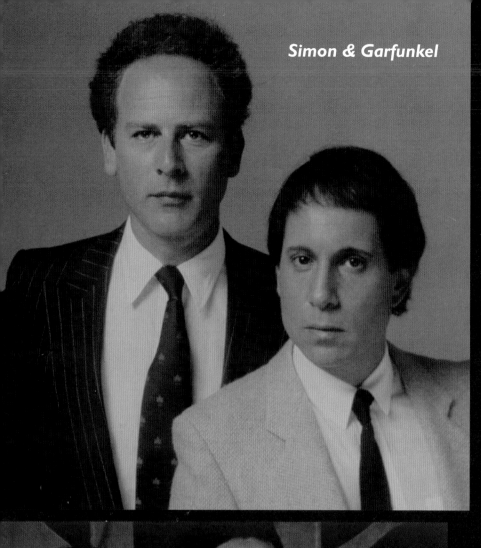
Simon & Garfunkel

Jim Morrison

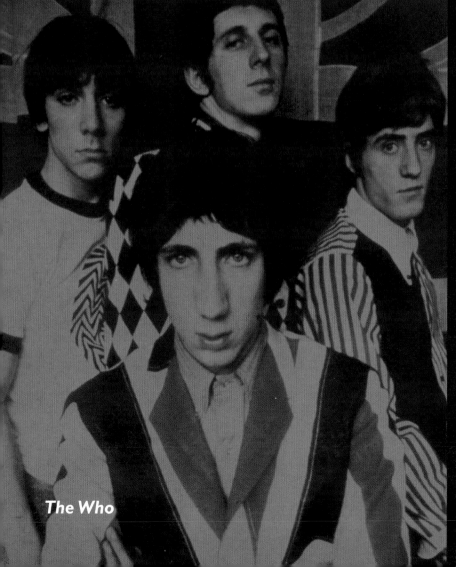
The Who

Gladys Knight and the Pips

CHAPTER 5

1967-1968

Viva La Revolution!

remember watching *The Graduate*, that great film from 1967, and being shocked, turned on, confused, and concerned. Come to think of it, that's pretty much how Dustin Hoffman's character, the young Ben Braddock, appears throughout most of the film. wasn't brought up the same way Ben was, but something about his struggle n a time of great transition resonated with me.

There's a very famous line from the movie that summarizes a whole generation's experience. Ben has just graduated college and a neighbor is giving him some unsolicited career

guidance. The advice comes in the form of a single word. *I want to say one word to you*, says the neighbor, Mr. McGuire. *Just one word. Are you listening? Plastics.*

Poor Ben is dumbfounded. Is this older man, this contemporary of his parents, really claiming to know what a twenty-one-year-old should do with his life? And could the best path really involve *plastic*—the symbol of everything phony and materialistic?

I now believe that this cinematic moment captured the divide between generations in 1967. Young people had a whole new set of idealistic expectations and spent much of the decade shaping

Strange Days, *1967*

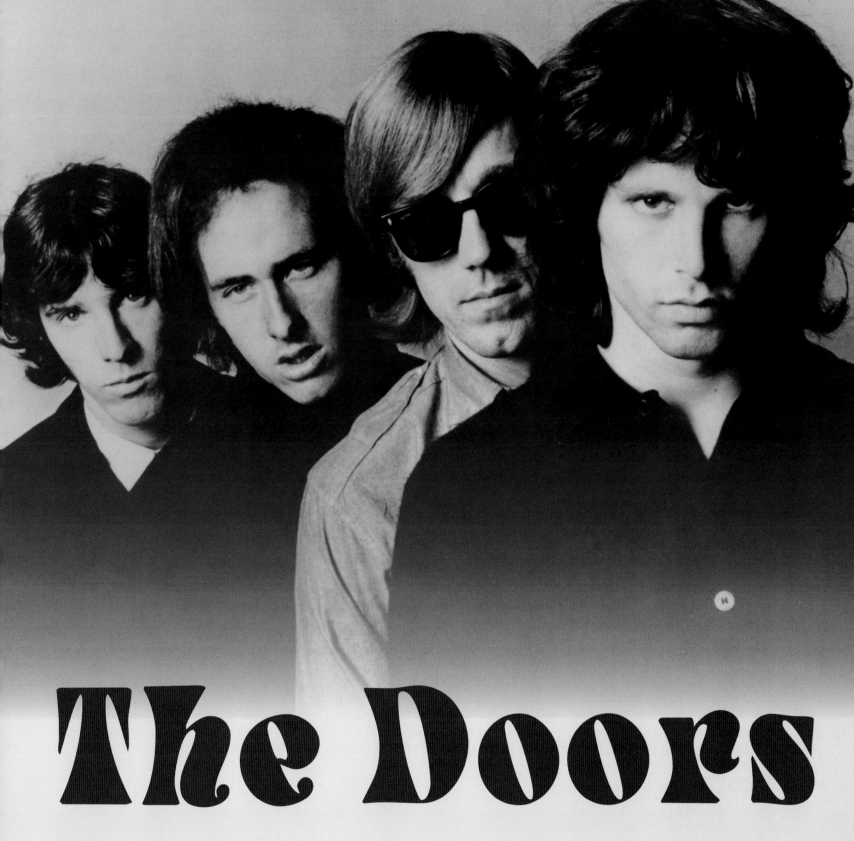

The Doors

Brooding and intense, with a controversy-courting frontman, the Doors hit number 1 with "Light My Fire" in 1967. They signaled the counterculture's shift from flower power to outright war against the establishment on Top 40 hits like "Riders on the Storm," "Touch Me," "People are Strange," and the chilling eleven-minute epic "The End."

CREAM

British power trio Cream was rock's first supergroup, combining Eric Clapton's fierce lead guitar with Jack Bruce's memorable bass lines and Ginger Baker's complex drumming. Not only did Cream deliver gigantic hits like "Sunshine of Your Love" and "White Room," they also set the blueprint for rock improvisation.

fresh ideas about a bright future in a better country. They didn't want the fake, plastic life their parents had lived. They had seen these failed role models accept everything the "establishment" sent down the pipeline. Racial segregation, joyless careers, the war in Vietnam, intelligent women tied down by apron strings—their parents drank it all down with a belt of Scotch. No, this generation was not going to take it without a fight. In fact, there was going to be a major war between the generations.

But the new generation had formed their revolutionary ideals in the cocoon of youth. Once they flew free, the contradictions of the adult world turned out to be very scary. They knew their parents were wrong, but they were confused and lost. As Simon and Garfunkel sang out on "Mrs. Robinson," the big hit from *The Graduate* soundtrack:

> *Laugh about it, shout about it*
> *When you've got to choose*
> *Every way you look at it you lose.*

The huge gap between generations of the 1960s was plain to see. And age was not the only thing separating people, either. By 1967, America was a nation divided along social, racial, political, and artistic lines. Within a year's time, the divisiveness would culminate in the tragedies of 1968.

It wasn't just Ben Braddock in *The Graduate*, but a whole nation that was coming of age in the second half of the decade. Even if you had your head in the sand, you couldn't escape the profound changes, because the sands were shifting.

By the way, I had the pleasure of finally meeting and dining with Mrs. Robinson—that is, the actress Anne Bancroft—in 2002. She was absolutely elegant and beautiful. All those years later, I still couldn't help thinking about her and that younger man (although actor Dustin Hoffman was only six years younger than Bancroft in "real life"). Deep down, cousins, I must confess that I couldn't help imagining myself as Ben.

Dressing the Part

The nation's youth may not have known where to turn in 1967, but they knew they wanted to put some serious mileage between themselves and the life laid out by the previous generation. Change, even just for the sake of change, became the new m.o. of young America. Change minds, change hair styles, change values—by any means necessary, they were going to change the status quo.

Even in radio, my own home territory, there were major transformations. AM radio had to start making room for FM programming, which was struggling

THE WAY HIPPIES DRESSED STRUCK FEAR INTO THE RULING CLASS.

VAN MORRISON

Van Morrison launched his lengthy career with "Brown Eyed Girl" in 1967. Over the decades, he's made intimate, meditative albums marrying folk, R&B, and jazz that have yielded enduring radio fare like "Domino," "Moondance," "Wild Night," and "Wavelength."

Judy Collins

Nothing less than royalty in the world of folk, Judy Collins is renowned and respected for her interpretations of well-loved songs like "Turn! Turn! Turn!" (by Pete Seeger), "I Think It's Going to Rain Today" (Randy Newman), and, perhaps most famously, "Both Sides Now" (Joni Mitchell). Judy also has a mesmerizing pair of peepers—and was the inspiration for the Crosby, Stills & Nash smash "Suite: Judy Blue Eyes."

Blue Cheer

This San Francisco trio was never destined for great chart success, but they were destined for rock & roll history. Hard-rock musicians remember their 1968 cover of "Summertime Blues" as the loudest thing they'd ever heard on record, and often credit Blue Cheer with cranking the heavy-metal machine into operation.

HAIR

Opens on Broadway

Er…make that *off* Broadway. The suits behind New York City's Great White Way still hadn't signed on to the idea that youth culture could draw a crowd—or at least not a desirable one—and initially declined to let the musical production *Hair* on their vaunted stages. But the producer's alternative setting, a renovated theater in the East Village, was closer to the creative heart of NYC anyway and mirrored the setting of the play.

Hair, the first rock musical, mixed all the core elements of 1967 youth culture. In the show, a group of urban bohemians known as the Tribe sing and dance their way through the issues of the day, from the Vietnam War to drug use to sexuality (a nude scene helped spark controversy…and publicity), while helping their friend Claude decide whether or not to dodge the draft.

Co-created by young actors James Rado and Gerome Ragni, with music by Galt MacDermot, the show not only mirrored the youth movement but became a part of it. Modern heroes like Janis Joplin could be spotted in the audience rocking out to "Aquarius" and "Let the Sunshine In."

Just six months after its October 1967 opening downtown, the businessmen uptown saw the light—or, more likely, saw the dollar signs. *Hair* opened at Broadway's Biltmore Theater in April of 1968.

1960s TV

By the 1960s, television had become so ingrained in our lives that few households didn't gather round to watch their favorite shows after dinner. The decade produced some terrific entertainment, with much of it still part of our pop culture consciousness.

Television in the 1960s had something for everyone, but it also started to tweak the "establishment" just like so many other parts of American popular culture were doing. *The Smothers Brothers Comedy Hour* was a perfect example. Designed as a variety show for the younger set, it starred brothers Tom and Dick Smothers, and had an anti-establishment theme that always pushed the network censors right to the wall. Eventually they just yanked it off the air after two seasons.

Rowan & Martin's Laugh-In fared much better. A goofy, groovy, and irreverent series of fast-paced comedy skits, the show launched the careers of Goldie Hawn, Lily Tomlin, Arte Johnson, and more. Other notable variety shows of the decade include *The Carol Burnett Show, The Dean Martin Show*, and *The Tonight Show* with Johnny Carson at the helm.

Star Trek is one of most successful pop culture franchises in television

Opposite Page: *Dick and Tom Smothers*
Above: *Leonard Nimoy and William Shatner explore the "final frontier" in Star Trek.*

history. The first voyage of the starship *Enterprise*, with William Shatner as Captain Kirk and Leonard Nimoy as Mr. Spock, went in search of the final frontier in 1966. Cancelled after three seasons, it later became an entertainment juggernaut through syndication, movies, television spin-offs, and a devoted fan base of "Trekkies," which continues today.

Situation comedies were all the rage. *The Monkees* were the American challenge to the Beatles while Fred MacMurray played dad on *My Three Sons*. A kooky group of castaways cavorted on *Gilligan's Island* and *The Beverly Hillbillies*

caused a stir in posh LA. Andy Griffith enjoyed a long run on *The Andy Griffith Show*, which starred Ron Howard as his son Opie, while Diahann Carroll finally broke another color barrier by playing an African American female lead who was not a stereotype in *Julia*. Meanwhile, Adam West, and an over-the-top production, made *Batman* an instant SMASH (see page 110).

There was no shortage of dramatic series with *The Mod Squad* going right for the counterculture crowd. Starring Michael Cole, Peggy Lipton, and Clarence Williams III as rebellious hippies turned cops, the show was a hit with kids.

There were also plenty of spy-themed shows to choose from (see page 126), and we watched the *Mission Impossible* team make it seem possible, the Cartwrights saddle up in *Bonanza,* David Janssen run for his life in *The Fugitive*, and Jack Lord cry "Book 'em Dano!" on *Hawaii Five-O.*

Michael Cole, Peggy Lipton, Tige Andrews and Clarence Williams III battle the bad guys in **The Mod Squad.**

Jefferson Airplane

Jefferson Airplane was the most commercially successful band to emerge from San Francisco's psychedelic rock scene. When she joined the band, ex-model Grace Slick brought the two songs—"White Rabbit" and "Somebody to Love"—that the Airplane turned into Top 10 hits on its chart-topping 1967 album *Surrealistic Pillow.*

SIMON AND GARFUNKEL

BOOKENDS/SIMON & GARFUNKEL

We tend to throw the term "poetry" around kind of liberally when talking about the lyrics of rock & roll songs. But every now and then, someone proves us right. The words Paul Simon created and put to music made for some of the most eloquent and poignant songs of our time.

Simon and childhood friend Art Garfunkel, who first performed as Tom and Jerry in the '50s, made for one of the most successful and well-loved duos of the late 1960s. Art's airy tenor lofted Paul's lyrics into the stratosphere, and together, their keen musical sensibilities made for an easy crossover from folk to pop and rock & roll. From 1965 to 1970, few months passed without a Simon & Garfunkel hit on the charts, including "Homeward Bound," "The Boxer," "Mrs. Robinson," and the stirring "Bridge Over Troubled Water," to name just a few.

for an audience at the time. Young FM programmers were formatting their shows for restless listeners who wanted to hear their own brand of rock & roll on the air. In its early years, FM radio really duplicated the programming of its AM big brother. But the FCC stepped in and "suggested"—and it was a strong-arm suggestion—that a certain percentage of FM programming could not be a mirror image of AM. As it would turn out in years to come, FM proved to be an ideal medium for the long song tracks and high-fidelity recordings released by rock artists.

Hippies were the poster children of change. We all have a version of the classic hippie image in mind; usually it's some variation on a barefoot, long-haired teenage kid wearing an embroidered shirt and beads around his neck. He's probably sitting cross-legged while strumming an acoustic guitar, or doing a free-form dance to some way-out music. Or maybe it's a fresh-faced California girl in a sundress with flowers in her hair.

Giving true meaning to the phrase "fashion statement," the way you wore yourself truly said something about your countercultural lifestyle. By sporting a

Change minds, change hair styles, change values...

beard or long hair, or by going totally uncoiffed, you could make an anti-establishment declaration—and freak out your parents—just by walking down the street. Vehement reactions from the older generation validated how effective fashion could be as a tool of rebellion. "Get a haircut!" they hollered. "You look like a girl!" "Take a shower!"

I'll always remember that, as if by magic, there was a sudden appearance of swirling colors and hypnotic patterns on album covers, like on *Days of Future Passed* by the Moody Blues or *Mellow Yellow* by Donovan. Those were the same explosions of color and life that young people were literally wearing on their sleeve. Though the growing legion of hippies was inherently pacifistic, the way they looked struck fear into the

The Grateful Dead

Bay Area rock collective the Grateful Dead were the pied pipers of the psychedelic revolution, taking audiences on musical trips by extending signature tunes like "Dark Star" into extended, fluid jams.

Young people poured into the Haight by the tens of thousands in the summer of '67.

ruling class. That fear, my cousins, wasn't the fear of a hairdo—it was the fear of *change*. Simply by rethinking the way they dressed and groomed themselves, young people were challenging the existing power structure.

Even though I was never a flower child myself, the hippie influence slowly but surely affected my own day-to-day duds. I remember pulling on my Beatle boots, buttoning up an ornate Edwardian shirt, strapping on a Union Jack necktie, and donning circular Ben Franklin glasses like the ones John Lennon used to wear. As I suited up for television appearances and stage shows, my costumes changed to fit the times.

Love and Haight

The epicenter of hippie lifestyle was the Haight-Ashbury district in San Francisco, California. Named for the intersection of Haight Street and Ashbury Street, "the Haight" in 1967 was a low-rent part of town where young people could afford some space, and they swung their doors open to friends and strangers alike. Once they made their way to the Haight, college students, drop-outs, runaways, and any other young bohemians could find cheap food, cheap drugs, and a floor (or a new friend) to sleep on.

Haight-Ashbury became a hippie mecca in June of 1967. When Scott McKenzie had a hit that summer with "San Francisco (Be Sure to Wear Flowers in Your Hair)," written by John Phillips of the Mamas & the Papas, the youth of the nation turned their sights westward. Phillips had penned the song to promote the Monterey Pop Festival, a three-day celebration of all things hippie. The festival featured performances by Jimi Hendrix, Janis Joplin, the Who, and

THE WHO

ARE THE KIDS REALLY ALRIGHT?

It seems appropriate that this band's name forms a question. It's as if someone is asking, Who in the world are these anti-establishment rockers, and why are they causing such a commotion? Does the character in "My Generation," their early signature song, have a stutter because he's insecure—or because he's on amphetamines? Was Keith Moon really out of it, or the most brilliant drummer of his time?

Another thing that had fans (and foes) scratching their heads was the band's smashing of their instruments. After doing his famous windmill strums on the guitar, Pete Townshend would send the neck of his guitar right into the huge stack of speakers behind him and knock over any part of the cabinet left standing. Moon would respond in kind, sending his kick drum and cymbals off the drum riser, and vocalist Roger Daltrey would swing his microphone around like a lasso. Only bassist John

Entwistle, the image of British aloofness, would stand fixed and undaunted on the stage.

Townshend has said the gear-bashing was inspired by Gustav Metzke, a painter who destroyed his own art as a form of social criticism. Townshend had attended art school in London and was tuned in to the fact that rock & roll had a visual power that could match its sonic power. If you look at all that the Who had going on onstage—lights and explosions, clothing bedecked with buttons and fringes, the giant Union Jack behind them, the smashing of guitars and drums, the smoking amplifiers—it was like a painting. The funny thing is that with such talent as songwriters, lyricists, and musicians, their music really required no backdrop to bring it to life. But when they hit the stage, the Who made graphic art.

GLADY'S KNIGHT & THE PIPS

Was there any sound more heartbreakingly romantic than a song by Gladys Knight & the Pips? If there was, I can't think of it. The group was a family affair from the very beginning, with the Pips made up of Gladys' brother Merald and cousins Edward Patten and William Guest. Another jewel in the Motown crown, the group broke through in 1967 with their version of "I Heard it Through the Grapevine" on Motown's subsidiary label, Soul. While many other R&B acts struggled to survive the transition out of the 1960s, Gladys Knight & the Pips changed labels and cemented their place in history with gorgeous, early-'70s super-hits like "Neither One of Us," "Midnight Train to Georgia" and "Best Thing That Ever Happened to Me."

WRITTEN ON THE WALLS

The New Age of Pop Art

Art broke the bounds of convention in the 1960s just like music did, exploding into a riot of color and fantasy. Influenced by Dadaists and drugs, New York artists like Andy Warhol, Peter Max, and Roy Lichtenstein turned soup cans and comic strips into hyper-real paintings that took the ordinary and made it mythic—reflecting the experience of turning on and tuning in. Meanwhile, in San Francisco, bands like the Grateful Dead and Moby Grape announced their gigs with psychedelic posters drawn by artists like Rick Griffin and Stanley Mouse & Alton Kelley, who mixed the ornate swirls of Art Nouveau and Victoriana with pop art's saturated colors and freaked-out hallucinogenic imagery. In 1968, the Beatles' animated feature *Yellow Submarine* introduced psychedelic art to the masses.

Kenny Rogers

This country music megastar recorded with the band First Edition before going solo in 1976. The group was popular in both the country- and pop-music circuits and topped the charts with singles like "Something Burning" and "Just Dropped In (to See What Condition My Condition Was In)," which peaked at number 5 in 1968.

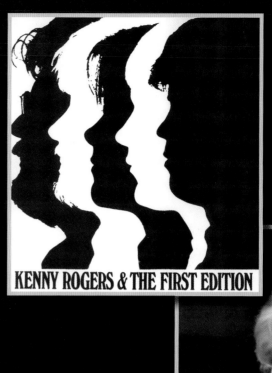

The Box Tops

This Memphis five-piece served up cool, blue-eyed soul, presaging artists like Hall & Oates. Singer Alex Chilton's earnest rasp drove "The Letter" to number 1 in 1967, and in '68 "Cry Like a Baby" was another huge international hit. Feeling fleeced by bad contracts, however, the Box Tops disbanded in 1970. Chilton went on to helm the critically acclaimed power-pop group Big Star.

The Democratic Convention of 1968

In 1968, 10,000 anti-war protestors converged on Chicago for the Democratic Convention—where frustration over the Vietnam War erupted in a bloody riot. Protests began humorously on August 23, with Yippie leaders Jerry Rubin and Abbie Hoffman holding a mock convention at which a pig was nominated for president. But on August 28, a rally exploded into violence when police broke through the crowd to beat a young boy who had lowered the American flag. Protestors pelted officers with rocks and food, and the police, unleashed by a furious Mayor Richard Daley, responded with tear gas and force. The violent atmosphere spilled into the convention hall, where even some respected journalists were roughed up by police rushing to quell demonstrations as they broke out.

The tide of Vietnam protests had given rise to the Anti-Riot Act of 1968, and someone's hide was going to be tanned for the convention protests. Hoffman, Rubin, and six others were indicted by a grand jury for inciting riot. Bobby Seale, one of the accused and a member of the Black Panther Party, caused such a scene in court that the judge ordered him bound and gagged, and eventually found him in contempt. With Seale sent off to prison (he received an unprecedented four-year sentence on charges of contempt), the activists on trial became known as the Chicago Seven. To many people it seemed like the whole resistance movement was on trial, and it became one of the most controversial and closely watched cases this country had ever seen. In the end, five of the seven were found guilty of violating the Anti-Riot Act.

Robert F. Kennedy

Robert F. Kennedy, center, with brothers John, left, and Ted, right

Like his brother, President John F. Kennedy, "Bobby" Kennedy was young, handsome, and had great hair. He was JFK's closest advisor and became US Attorney General at age thirty-six, a post he kept under President Lyndon Johnson after Kennedy's assassination in '63. RFK fearlessly tackled the American mafia and corrupt Teamsters president Jimmy Hoffa, and stringently enforced the new Civil Rights Act his brother had championed. RFK broke with Johnson over the Vietnam War, and became a US Senator in 1965. He was close to winning the Democratic party nomination for president when he was fatally shot by Sirhan Sirhan in '68. The outpouring of public grief was so intense that Johnson declared a national day of mourning—and all presidential candidates since have been assigned security details.

For those who were truly on the front lines of change, things weren't so groovy at all.

Indian sitarist Ravi Shankar, but the people who gathered at the fairgrounds in Monterey weren't there to be an audience of spectators—they came to be together. Monterey Pop, which lasted from June 16 through June 18, 1967, kicked off the Summer of Love.

I visited the Haight three times in 1967 and 1968 to film special TV features. The camaraderie of the people there impressed me greatly.

I'll never forget one early morning when a huge line had formed outside the Fillmore West, where Jefferson Airplane was to perform that night. The Fillmore West, along with its companion venue the Fillmore East in New York, was one of the hottest rock & roll concert stages in the country. At about 8:00 that morning, Fillmore promoter Bill Graham and Jefferson Airplane vocalist Grace Slick invited me to join them in handing out apples to everyone waiting in line. We passed out basket after basket of green apples to all the fans waiting in line. And I have to tell you, it was the most patient and gracious group of fans I've ever seen. Those kids would wait another twelve hours before the show began, but they kept the peace. I guess an apple a day keeps the anger away.

Young people poured into the Haight by the tens of thousands in the summer of '67. Though similar movements were afoot in cities all over the nation (and in a few European cities as well), San Francisco became ground zero for the cultural renaissance of the '60s. A living soundtrack provided by San Fran natives like Jefferson Airplane and the Grateful Dead set the background for a sunny summer of free expression. It was everything the young generation could hope for: liberation from the

Music held up a mirror to the entire range of emotion brought about by those difficult days.

confines of their parents' four walls, but with the comfort and protection of a huge community. For the hippies of Haight-Ashbury, there was safety in numbers…and, for some, in hallucinogenic escape.

Searching for New Sounds

Newly empowered and emboldened, the youth movement thrived creatively. Musical artists were becoming more adventuresome as they freed themselves from convention, and rock & roll was splitting and splintering in all new directions. Mind-expanding experiments of all sorts led to heavy, heady music. 1967 saw the debut of groundbreaking artists like the Doors (featuring singer Jim Morrison's psycho-sexual lyrics); Jimi Hendrix (with the albums *Axis: Bold As Love* and *Are You Experienced*); and

Cream, the world's first "supergroup," which included guitarist Eric Clapton in the driver's seat, Jack Bruce on bass and vocals, and Ginger Baker on drums.

As you may know, Jim Morrison was quite a character, and stories about him have already filled a few memorable books. My own favorite encounter with Jim came when I was doing a television report on the Doors for NBC TV News. I had arrived at the very elegant Delmonico Hotel on Park Avenue in New York with my camera crew. Jim and I met in the restaurant of this very staid and conservative hotel, and he had been sitting politely for most of the interview. From out of nowhere, he jumped up from the table, ran out to Park Avenue and started running after a taxicab! I told the crew to follow me and we chased him down Park Avenue.

Vanilla Fudge

Vanilla Fudge gave the Supremes song "You Just Keep Me Hanging On" the psychedelic hard-rock treatment in 1967, slowing it down and adding washes of organ. The cover was Vanilla Fudge's first Top 10 hit.

STEPPENWOLF

The term "heavy metal" is often credited to the lyric "heavy metal thunder" from this Canadian rock band's hit "Born to Be Wild." More hard-rock than heavy metal in their own right, Steppenwolf was led by vocalist John Kay and found success with guitar-driven singles like "Magic Carpet Ride" and "Rock Me."

Aretha Franklin

The long-reigning Lady Soul first introduced her gospel-heavy soul music to the masses in 1967 with *I Never Loved a Man (The Way I Love You)*, a remarkably powerful album yielding big hits with the title cut and "Respect." Tender one moment and tough as nails the next, every melody graced by her singular voice—from "Think" to "Chain of Fools" to "I Say a Little Prayer"—the album was a powerful shot to the heart. Aretha appealed to very broad audiences, but was a special source of pride among African Americans during and after the Civil Rights Movement.

R-E-S-P-E-C-T!
Find out what it means to me!

When he finally caught up with the cab at a traffic light, Morrison started kicking the taxi's trunk and shouting utterances that even Cousin Brucie couldn't use on television. Then, as suddenly as the episode had started, Jim calmed down, returned to the safety of the Delmonico, and continued the interview as if nothing had happened. Cousins, I don't know what he had for breakfast that morning, but it wasn't the same thing on my plate.

In bands like the Doors and others like them, rock music started to feature a lot of trippy lyrics and extended guitar solos. The style was moving on from the innocent, danceable sound heard on earlier work by artists such as the Beatles. In fact, even the Beatles were moving away from the Beatles. That's why their landmark 1967 album was called *Sgt. Pepper's Lonely Hearts Club Band*. With that title they were assuming a new identity: As the Lonely Hearts Club Band, and not the world-famous Beatles, they could try something new without being held down to old expectations about who they were and what they should sound like.

Even the cover of *Sgt. Pepper* carries the message that the band wanted to leave its familiar identity behind. Standing next to the real John, Ringo, Paul, and George are the statues of the Fab Four from Madame Tussaud's. The "old" Beatles were consigned to history along with all the other faces behind them. Ever notice that the whole scene on that album cover is a gravesite? Talk about burying your past. The name "Beatles" is spelled out in flowers on the fresh dirt.

The music on *Sgt. Pepper* fulfilled the promise of a reborn band, too. After countless mega-concerts in which they couldn't even hear themselves play above screaming fans, the guys had made a firm decision to end their run

Movies Explore Antiheroes, Outlaws, Tough Guys, and Teenage Angst

Anne Bancroft gives Dustin Hoffman some extracurricular advice in The Graduate.

I have discussed *The Graduate* with Dustin Hoffman as Ben Braddock, the unlikely antihero of the moment (see page 159) but there were many stars who were portraying guys who did it their way. Steve McQueen was the king of cool, either romancing Faye Dunaway in *The Thomas Crown Affair* or Jacqueline Bisset in *Bullitt*.

Paul Newman's cocky inmate in *Cool Hand Luke* caused his jailer to drawl, "What we have here is a failure to communicate." He later teamed with Robert Redford and Katherine Ross in *Butch Cassidy and the Sundance Kid*, which was a hit across all age groups.

Meanwhile, 1967's *Bonnie and Clyde* was a celebration of the ultimate anti-establishment duo. With Warren Beatty and Faye Dunaway in the lead roles,

Sidney Poitier tames a London classroom in **To Sir with Love.**

there were never two more glamorous gangsters. Their demise in a hail of bullets and blood still provides a jolt today. By this time, sexuality and violence in movies was starting to be more graphic and the motion picture industry adopted a rating system to cue moviegoers as to content. We still have it today. By the way, cousins, R stands for "Really Sexy."

The Wild Bunch, Sam Peckinpah's classic western about a group of aging outlaws, starring William Holden and Ernest Borgnine, upped the ante on slow motion movie violence, while *In Cold Blood,* based on the best-selling book, starred Robert Blake and Scott Wilson. Filmed in black and white, it is a gritty docudrama about the slaughter of a Kansas family.

Many movies from across the pond were exploring class struggles and "angry young men," but Hollywood took on the troubles of inner-city London in *To*

Warren Beatty and Faye Dunaway shoot up the big screen in **Bonnie and Clyde.**

Sir with Love. Starring Sidney Poitier as a dedicated teacher who finds a way to reach his bored and rebellious students, the movie also starred Judy Geeson and featured Lulu singing the title song.

I am glad to say that there was also room for love stories in the cynical 1960s, and Franco Zeffirelli's excellent version of Shakespeare's *Romeo and Juliet* captivated audiences. Stars Leonard Whiting and Olivia Hussey were only teenagers during the movie shoot, which would have pleased the Bard, and its main theme, "A Time for Us," was a hit as well. Then there was *Bob & Carol & Ted & Alice* (yes, that is how the title actually read), which explored the "fashionable" new wave of sexual freedom.

Doomed lovers Olivia Hussey and Leonard Whiting in Romeo and Juliet.

Celebrity Couples

Sinatra & Mia, Elvis & Priscilla, Liz & Dick

Elizabeth Taylor and Richard Burton in **The Comedians**

Celebrity marriages were almost as entertaining as the movies. Actress Mia Farrow married singer Frank Sinatra in 1966 when she was twenty-one and he was fifty. She agreed to appear in his 1968 film *The Detective* but reneged when filming for *Rosemary's Baby* ran over. Sinatra responded by serving Farrow divorce papers in front of her cast and crew.

The marriage between Elvis and Priscilla Presley was shorter than their eight-year courtship, begun when Priscilla was fourteen. After marrying in 1967, they separated in 1972.

Elizabeth Taylor and Richard Burton fell hard while filming *Cleopatra*, and quickly shed their respective marriages. Despite Vatican charges of "erotic vagrancy," Taylor married Burton in '64. They made movies together, drank like fish, and fought like tigers. The couple split in 1974 and remarried a year later. The rematch lasted just four months. As Burton observed, "For some reason the world has always been amused by us two maniacs."

Young people didn't want the fake plastic life their parents had lived.

as a live band, and performed their last show at San Fran's Candlestick Park in 1966. Drawing heavily on inspiration from the Beach Boys' *Pet Sounds*, the boys from Liverpool then turned their talents to creating songs that utilized modern recording technology to the fullest extent. In fact, recording techniques were significantly advanced as Lennon and McCartney, aided by genius recording professionals like engineer Geoff Emerick and producer George Martin, conducted wild sonic experiments in the studio.

The greatest example from *Sgt. Pepper* is the song I consider their ultimate masterpiece, "A Day in the Life." The song opens with a small-group arrangement, then swells with the accompaniment of a full forty-piece orchestra. Committing all of those strings and brass to tape—and adding them on top of the instruments played by the Beatles themselves—tested the recording capacity of Abbey Road Studios and the creativity of all the people working behind the console. Then the whole *Sgt. Pepper* album culminates in that thunderous piano chord at the end of the song. Actually, it was one chord pounded out simultaneously on three pianos by four musicians, and sustained for more than a minute! What a sound.

Sgt. Pepper is frequently regarded as the greatest album in rock & roll. But one curious note is that a lot of people have referred to it as rock's seminal "concept" record. I've always taken issue with that. What concept links all of those songs together? What does "Lucy in the Sky with Diamonds" have to do with "When I'm Sixty-Four"? Nothin', far as I can tell. Just because they created musical segues between songs doesn't mean there was any conceptual link among the tracks. The only thing all the songs on *Sgt. Pepper* have in common is that they're flippin' fantastic.

THE BEE GEES

British brothers Barry, Maurice, and Robin Gibb had an uncannily beautiful blend of voices that enabled the Bee Gees to become one of the most successful vocal groups of all time. They segued smoothly from Beatles-ish pop in the '60s to become architects of disco with their unforgettable later contributions to the *Saturday Night Fever* soundtrack in 1977. The album sold over 40 million copies and gave the Bee Gees a string of number 1 hits including "You Should Be Dancing," "Stayin' Alive," and "Night Fever."

STEVE WINWOOD

A wunderkind at fifteen and now a distinguished elder statesman at sixty, Steve Winwood has had a diverse career as band member and solo artist over the past forty years. Winwood first showcased his vocal and keyboard talents as a teenager in the Spencer Davis Group on "Gimme Some Lovin'" and "I'm a Man." He formed Traffic ("The Low Spark of High-Heeled Boys") in 1967, and in 1969 teamed with guitarist Eric Clapton and drummer Ginger Baker for the short-lived Blind Faith, which released a single, superb record (*Blind Faith* yielding "Can't Find My Way Home" and others).

At five minutes and five seconds long, "A Day in the Life" would never have been heard on the airwaves were it not for the changes to FM radio. On the mainstream AM band, limiting song plays to two-and-a-half minutes was not just common practice—it was the law. Promotional copies of long tunes like the Doors' "Light My Fire" would be cut down to 2:30 so that we could play *most* of the hit and then cut away to a commercial. But on FM, a hip radio personality could say, "Hey listeners, let's smoke a banana and dig this seven-minute album cut." An entire faction of radio, like newspapers, was coming up from underground. More and more, FM stations became the voice of unrest.

A War of Worlds

It wasn't long after the release of *Sgt. Pepper* that the Beatles and several of their contemporaries traveled to India to meet with a guru known as Maharishi. The whole hippie movement had spiritual leanings, and the idea of pursuing transcendental thought—by meditating with or without the help of some transcendental drugs—seemed to appeal to a lot of people. Hippies had been encouraging one another to resist the material trappings of the Western world, and it seemed to be increasingly popular to go gaga for a guru.

For those who were truly on the front lines of change, things weren't so groovy at all. As boyfriends, brothers, and sons lost their lives and limbs on the actual front lines of war in Vietnam, anti-war sentiment was reaching a boiling point here at home. By 1968 we had well over half a million of our boys fighting a battle many believed was wrongly rooted in greed and imperialism. Some demonstrations against Vietnam were entirely peaceful; others were based on civil disobedience; still others began peaceful and turned violent. At those massive marches and "teach-ins" you could often hear demonstrators singing the protest songs that gave voice to the opposition: songs like "White Boots Marching in a Yellow Land" and "The War Is Over" by Phil Ochs, "Sky Pilot" by the Animals, and the "I-Feel-Like-I'm-Fixin'-to-Die Rag" by Country Joe and the Fish. Also known as "The Fish Cheer," Country Joe would lead enthusiastic audiences through a not-so-cheery chorus of *1 2 3, what are*

Tommy James and the Shondells

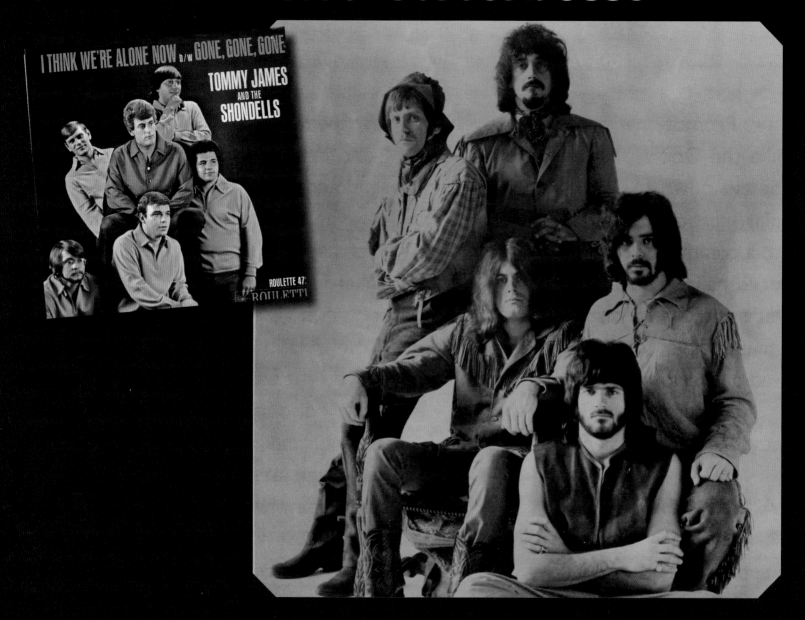

Tommy James and the Shondells turned out one hit after another between 1967 and 1969, including six that reached the Top 10: "I Think We're Alone Now," "Mirage," "Mony Mony," "Crimson and Clover," "Sweet Cherry Wine," and "Crystal Blue Persuasion." Declining to play Woodstock on the advice of their agent, who thought it would be bad for their career, the Shondells split up in 1970. Rocker Joan Jett, managed by former Shondell Kenny Laguna, had a top 10 hit with "Crimson and Clover" in 1982.

we fighting for? People came to expect nothing other than protest songs when Country Joe took the stage.

The war was another razor, a deep and cutting blade, in the side of America's youth. For many, it was proof that our leadership was out of synch with its own people. As always, music held up a mirror to the entire range of emotion brought about by those difficult days, and the Top 100 songs of 1968 represented feelings all across the spectrum. There were peace-loving tunes like "Love Is All Around" by the Troggs and "(Sittin' On) The Dock of the Bay" by Otis Redding. Consoling songs like "Hey Jude" co-existed on the chart with rebel rousers like Steppenwolf's "Born to Be Wild." For everyone who wanted to tune out all the bad vibes, there were plenty of spacey psychedelic songs, such as "Stoned Soul Picnic" by the Fifth Dimension and "Hurdy Gurdy Man" by Donovan. Then there were the melancholy numbers like "Galveston," the gorgeous song by Jimmy Webb (and sung by Glen Campbell) in which a soldier pines for his Texas hometown and wonders if his girl is still waiting for him there: *While I watch the cannons flashing / I clean my gun / And dream of Galveston.*

For those of my cousins who remember World War II songs like the Andrews Sisters' "Don't Sit Under the Apple Tree" or Vaughn Monroe's "When the Lights Go on Again All Over the World," the theme of a returning soldier will be a familiar one. It seems that every war inspires images of home.

What's Goin' On?

Rock & roll is so full of life, happiness, and hope—it's the very definition of "upbeat." It's almost painful to think of that positive spirit taking the beating that it did in the 1960s, but that's what the people and their music were up against. We were all so confused. We knew there was something more out there but had no clue how to find it. Certainly our leaders weren't pointing the way, and the most crushing blows came when those rare heroes did emerge—only to be cut down. There had been hope for a united nation back in the early '60s, when John F. Kennedy made young and old alike feel like they had something to believe in. His assassination in 1963 was the end of a dream. The vision of a better

Pop Goes the Bubblegum

Ohio Express

While folkies and rock & rollers were writing heady songs that examined and challenged society, something different was going on with "bubblegum" pop—a style named as much for its super-sweet style as the gum-chewin' teenyboppers it appealed to widely. The bands blowing bubbles of pink pop in the '60s included the Lemon Pipers with "Green Tambourine," 1910 Fruitgum Company with "1, 2, 3 Red Light" and "Simon Says," and the Ohio Express with "Yummy, Yummy, Yummy."

It's not hard to see why a lyric like *Yummy, yummy, yummy, I've got love in my tummy* didn't do much to advance the era's intellectual causes. But the songs did appeal to our need for escapism and had a core quality of providing comfort and familiarity. Whether or not you had a sweet tooth for these little confections, they had the markings of any successful pop song: a simple chord progression and a catchy melodic "hook" to catch listeners. That's why the style endured for years, influencing later bubble-blowers like the Archies and the Banana Splits, and detectable in the super-poppy elements of punk artists like the Ramones.

Women's Liberation

I grew up in a home with old fashioned values. My father and his father went out to work and my mom and grandmother stayed home and took care of us kids. I guess I thought this was the way it should be, but I am glad to say that by the 1960s I knew that it wasn't right for all women. The extraordinary people I knew, and the social upheavals of the times, made us realize that options and choices are for all of us, not just a select group. If you choose to stay home, fine, but if you want to go out in the world and be a musician, politician, or president, that should be fine as well.

There has been a battle of the sexes since cavemen and cavewomen started arguing about who was bringing home the woolly mammoth, but the feminist movement had two great surges between the late nineteenth century and the 1970s. The first secured the vote. Yes, it's hard to believe that it wasn't till 1920 that every US state "granted" women the right to vote. The other, ignited in the 1960s by a group of dedicated feminists

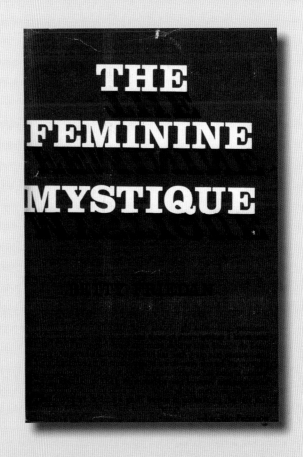

like Betty Friedan and Gloria Steinem, was focused on equality. That meant campaigning for the freedom to make safe, personal decisions about sex and reproduction, equal pay for equal work, political representation, and more.

Everyone remembers activists burning their bras, and for a time it was very fashionable to not wear one. I don't think us guys had any problem with that. I will say that no matter who you are, striving for equality is part of being American and I hope it stays that way.

nation had arisen from the ashes when his brother Robert F. Kennedy made a run for president. But the revived dream was dashed again by an assassin's bullet in 1968.

For a time it seemed like we just couldn't keep the nation knitted together, and with the assassination that same year of Martin Luther King, Jr., we were nearly torn completely apart. In MLK, so many of the things that separated people—factors of race, socioeconomics, religion, war, politics—were ready to fall. But instead it was King who fell, and the walls stood. When we lost that man, it was like the whole passive resistance movement was out of steam. There were riots in over 100 cities, including devastating displays of anger in Detroit, Washington, DC, and Newark, New Jersey.

In a few banner moments, though, music rode in to the rescue. James Brown, the Godfather of Soul, had been scheduled to play a concert to 14,000 people in Boston on the night after King was shot. Boston, a city with deep racial divisions, seemed ready to blow. City leaders were panicked that a concert hall full of young African Americans would be a flashpoint for a riot that could spread like wildfire. But following a heartfelt speech by Boston's left-leaning mayor, Kevin White, the Godfather took the stage. When tensions between fans and police started to flare, James Brown kept everybody cool. He cleared the stage of unruly fans and aggressive cops and then asked, "Now, are we together or we ain't?"

The band kicked back in, and Boston kept the peace that night.

In Martin Luther King, so many of the walls that separated people were ready to fall.

Newfound Respect

Relations were strained between genders as well. Young women everywhere were railing against traditional views and social customs that objectified and restricted them. The so-called gentler gender began rallying behind leaders like feminist crusader Betty Friedan, who had fueled a new women's movement with the release of her book *The Feminine Mystique*. A study by sex researchers Masters and Johnson, first released in 1966, shattered misconceptions about female sexuality, and now women everywhere were recovering power over their own bodies and minds. Everything that confined women was going up in flames as they burned their bras in a show of physical and psychological liberation.

The women's movement had its own momentum, but rock & roll had a hand in pushing it forward. One of the greatest feminist moments in music has to be Aretha Franklin's recording of "Respect." The tune had been written and recorded by Otis Redding. Otis had a great rendition, of course, and in his voice the song was a fairly traditional take on a man asking for his partner's "respect" when he returns home from

The Stooges

The Stooges were pioneers of the aggressive sound that would become known as punk rock. Despite negative response from the critics and the mainstream alike, the band was undeniably groundbreaking. Frontman Iggy Pop, once reviled for his ferocious performances, has in retrospect been revered as an innovator.

Roddy McDowall and Kim Hunter go ape over Charlton Heston in **Planet of the Apes.**

FANTASY AND HORROR FILMS

Fantasy and horrors films have been around since we first started going into movie theaters for a few hours of escapism. However, both genres began to flex their muscles in the 1960s.

Science fiction was big in the 1950s, but with few exceptions, the special effects were not very sophisticated. That all changed in 1968 with Stanley Kubrick's *2001: A Space Odyssey*,

which paved the way for the next generation of special effects masters and the galactic space operas to follow. Combining classical music and stunning imagery with an ambiguous storyline, it brought outer space into our space. However as space people go, I have to admit, it is Jane Fonda in *Barbarella* that caught my cosmic attention.

Using extraordinary makeup techniques, *Planet of the Apes*, starring Charlton Heston and Roddy McDowall, brought us closer to our simian cousins—maybe too close. Many sequels followed the film, but the last shot of the original, which shows the Statue of Liberty in the place she should not be, is a classic. Other notables of the time are *Fahrenheit 451* starring Oscar Werner as a "fireman" who burns books in this ugly, alternative view of the future, and *Fantastic Voyage* which shrinks stars

Jane Fonda gets spacey in Barbarella.

Mia Farrow has an unusual offspring in **Rosemary's Baby**

and Alfred Hitchcock was having fun in the shower (see page 90).

It was waiflike Mia Farrow in *Rosemary's Baby* who expertly brought horror to a more mainstream audience. Married to an aspiring actor, played by John Cassavetes, Rosemary has devil worshipers for neighbors and that's just the start of her trouble, poor girl. On the other end of the spectrum, *Night of the Living Dead* was a no-budget ghoulish gore-fest that pushed all the envelopes at the time. It was not my thing, but many people loved it. (Cousins, I have to say that in case any ghouls are reading this.)

Raquel Welch and Stephen Boyd to microscopic size to perform an operation in someone's bloodstream. Strange premise but remember, nano is the word!

Horror films and thrillers came in all guises. Vincent Price was still teaming up with director Roger Corman in films like *The Masque of the Red Death* while Bette Davis and Joan Crawford were having a field day in *What Ever Happened to Baby Jane? The Haunting,* starring Julie Harris, was an understated creeper

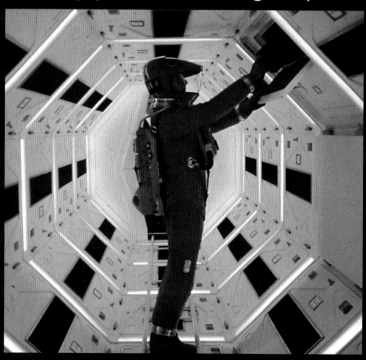

Keir Dullea in **2001: A Space Odyssey**

a hard day's work. But Aretha swapped the gender roles when she sang the song and turned it completely on its head. She offered a lyric that never even appeared on Otis' original, and sang it out with the strength of a million fed-up women: *R-E-S-P-E-C-T, find out what it means to me / R-E-S-P-E-C-T, take care, TCB!* That "TCB" was short for "taking care of business"—and boy, was Aretha doing her job for women everywhere.

Contrasts and Contradictions

What a miraculous, strange, and terrible time it was. We were a nation split into different sides, in a dozen bewildering ways. There were militant crackdowns on protesters, but hippies were dropping flowers down the gun barrels of federal marshals. It was the dawn of the liberal age, but conservative California governor Richard Nixon was elected president. Racial tensions exploded, but the 1968 Civil Rights Act was passed (and would later prove to be the first step on a long, rocky road). We couldn't get our own world in order, but astronauts flew near the moon and circled it ten times! The space race between the Soviet Union and the USA was just one of the many tension-builders in the topsy-turvy world of the '60s.

It was a time of great contradiction and of great change. Though our nation's young people were finding their way to one another, it's fair to say they were still collectively lost. It had taken a lot to separate themselves from the adult world, and now they found themselves in the woods. History has remembered those hippie days very affectionately, yet in truth, there were both real advocates for a better world and a huge portion of the young population that was just overly self-indulgent and irresponsible—a portion of the crowd I like to say had "unrest without zest."

But the loudest, most effective voices among them were shouting *STOP THE MADNESS*. Through their art, their fashion, their marches, and their music, the youth of the late 1960s were shifting the country's distribution of power. Everything they stood for and sang for would truly revolutionize America.

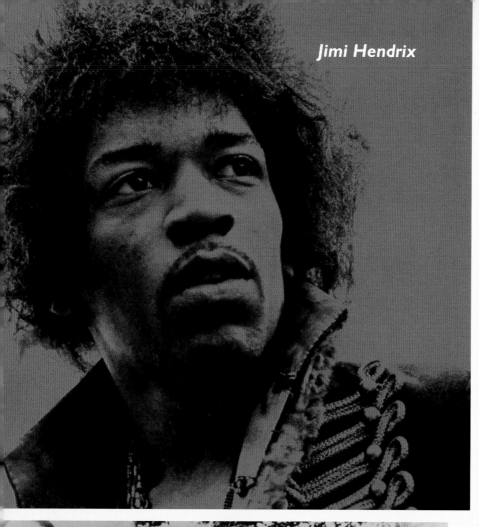

Jimi Hendrix

Creedence
Clearwater
Revival

Crosby, Stills, Nash & Young
with Dallas Taylor and Greg Reeves

Neil Diamond

CHAPTER 6

1969

In the Rock Garden

The Nobel Prize committee has never nominated me for a science award, but there are one or two laws of physics I know to be true.

An object in motion will stay in motion unless something stops it, as Sir Isaac Newton taught me (or was it his great grandson, Fig?). The same goes for human beings: People will continue on a given path unless someone or something stands in the way.

Even with many obstacles facing the youth revolution, it was still hurtling forward at the end of the 1960s. It had been an unprecedented time of motion and unrest, and by the last year of the decade our society was still propelled by the momentum of change. Without a doubt, in 1969 we were still a long way from resolving the countless issues that had been churned up. A decade that had been all about searching and uncertainty had to end with a question mark.

To the older generation it may have seemed like a lot of change just for the sake of change, but in truth the unrest was caused by spiritual and intellectual hunger. You could see it in the streets, you could read it in the papers, and you could especially hear it in the music. There was no going back to the neat and clean doo wop era of the 1950s,

Jimi Hendrix

Known by the masses as the greatest guitarist ever, Jimi Hendrix flashed across the late '60s like a comet across the sky. In just four years—from his 1967 debut *Are You Experienced* until his passing in 1970 at the age of 27—Hendrix changed the world's idea of what was possible on an electric guitar. While he's remembered for "acid rock" hits like "Purple Haze" and a great take on Bob Dylan's "All Along the Watchtower," Jimi revealed the gentler spirit of his nature on exceptionally pretty tunes like "Castles Made of Sand" and "Angel."

MONTEREY POP
and the First Rock Festivals

*Three days of "Peace and Music" on Yasgur's farm,
from the movie* **Woodstock**

When the Beatles sold out Shea Stadium in 1965, it changed everyone's mind about just how big a rock & roll show could get. For music fans, a festival featuring a revolving roster of top rock & roll performers was an opportunity to enjoy music in the communal spirit of the day. Early rock fests were as much about hearing live music as expressing yourself with 50,000 of your closest friends.

The Monterey International Pop Festival was a three-day happening in the Summer of Love. From June 16 to 18, 1967, some 200,000 fans overtook the Monterey County Fairgrounds to catch a mixed bag of cross-continental talent. The show was a charity event with an entrance fee of just one dollar, and of the more than thirty performing artists—including the Who, the Grateful Dead, Jimi Hendrix (in his first major American performance), Simon and Garfunkel, and Otis Redding—only one was paid. Ravi

Grace Slick of Jefferson Airplane from the documentary **Monterey Pop.**

Shankar was supposedly compensated $3,000, and gave an exceptionally long performance on his sitar. With due respect to Ravi, some fans might have paid a few bucks to shorten the set.

Monterey set the stage (so to speak) for festivals to come, and several soon followed in Miami, Atlanta, Denver, and elsewhere. But the two biggies were the Woodstock Music and Arts Festival in upstate New York and the Altamont Free Concert at the old Altamont Speedway east of San Francisco. Woodstock was arguably the defining moment of 1960s youth culture and, despite many criticisms from conservative America, was a peaceful tribute to love and music in August of '69 (read more about my own Woodstock experience starting on page 231). But Altamont, held that same year on December 6, was a disaster. One of the bands—some say it was the Rolling Stones, others say the Grateful Dead—hired the Hell's Angels to provide security detail, a job the notorious gang accepted for a payment of free beer. Performances by the likes of Santana; Jefferson Airplane; and Crosby, Stills, & Nash went off well, but trouble started brewing during the Stones' set. You can watch the movie *Gimme Shelter* and decide for yourself what happened or who was at fault, but a young black man named Meredith Hunter, who had a gun and was near the stage, was stabbed by one of the Hell's Angels. He didn't make it out of Altamont alive.

The violence at Altamont provided exactly what the youth movement's detractors needed to validate their view that rock & roll was played by and for a degenerate generation. For the rest of us, it was an isolated and terribly sad exception to the rule.

The Cowsills

The wholesome Cowsill family from Rhode Island—six siblings and their mom—sang intricate four- and five-part harmonies on million-selling hits like "Indian Lake" in 1968 and a recording of the title song from *Hair* in 1969. They were the real-life models for the Partridge Family.

when the angst and urgency that young people felt remained in the closet.

Now Hear This

All over the charts you could detect a new intensity and depth of passion. Blood, Sweat & Tears, led by keyboardist Al Kooper, matched earnest rock vocals with R&B horns—and a great sense of pop chops—in tunes like "Spinning Wheel" and "You've Made Me So Very Happy." Creedence Clearwater Revival had a muscular, no-nonsene hit with "Proud Mary," which would later get a completely different read by Ike & Tina Turner. There was pure joy on a song like "Build Me Up Buttercup" by the Foundations, then touching and lonely compositions like "Wichita Lineman" sung by Glen Campbell and "I Started a Joke" by the Bee Gees. Even in gentle songs like "He Ain't Heavy, He's My Brother" by the Hollies (which featured a young Elton John on piano) there was a soulful cry to be heard and understood.

Due in part to the loss of Martin Luther King, Jr. in 1968, R&B artists had come to the national foreground and were riding on the success of their biggest year. They were producing some of the most endearing and enduring songs of our time in 1969, including greats like "For Once in My Life" (Stevie Wonder), "Heard It Through the Grapevine" (Marvin Gaye), "What Does It Take (To Win Your Love)" (Junior Walker and the All-Stars), and "I'm Gonna Make You Love Me" (a dual effort by the Supremes and the Temptations).

Just by reading the song titles you can hear those wonderful melodies and rhythms echoing in your mind. There's a common denominator in R&B music that seems to strike a chord in us all. To me, it's the poetic heart and soul of humanity. Great R&B is palatable to nearly everyone, perhaps because no matter what is happening around us, the songs tell a very basic human story. Regardless of what we're going through politically, racially, or otherwise, R&B reaches through and touches us. It's all about the everyday adventures of the human spirit. Sly & the Family Stone said it best when they wrote a song we could all sing along to, and sang *I am everyday people*. And you know, there was also some wisdom in the words of Funkadelic when they sang, *Free your mind and your ass will follow*!

A decade that had been all about searching and uncertainty had to end with a question mark.

Rock & Roar

Rock & roll had always been a good excuse to exorcise one's inner demons—even if the establishment thought we were all listening to "devil's music." But as the music echoed ever more troublesome times, it began taking the form of a howl from deep inside.

A number of earth-shaking recordings from 1969 sounded like releases of youthful energy in its purest form.

Walking on the Moon

Having a man walk on the moon was the realization of a dream. Not just the dream of John F. Kennedy, who in 1961 said we should set our sights on "landing a man on the Moon and returning him safely to Earth" before the decade was out. It had been the dream of poets, visionaries, romanticists, and anyone else who had looked into the night sky since the dawn of time.

On July 20, 1969, millions stared at the grainy television images with their jaws on the floor—including your Cousin Brucie, who was watching the event with friend Neil Sedaka. Science fiction came to life in front of us as a camera mounted to the side of Apollo 11 captured Commander Neil Armstrong walking on the powdery surface of the moon. Lunar module pilot "Buzz" Aldrin soon joined Armstrong, and the two went to work planting an American flag. In the original footage, you can see Aldrin doing a two-footed hop in the lunar gravity, and he looks something like a kindergarten kid bouncing around a schoolyard. It was like an expression of the pure joy we all were feeling.

Accomplishing the mission at the tail end of the turbulent '60s made it a kind of bittersweet success, to my mind. It showed the miraculous potential of the human race while at the same time revealing how misguided and lost we were back on our own planet. We could literally touch the soil of another world—yet back home we were picking fights over race, color, and creed. Apollo 11 was a mission of hope. Why couldn't we achieve such lofty goals here on terra firma?

A year after his lunar landing, Armstrong told the *New York Times* that he had hoped this incredible achievement would help the world put all of its

problems in a new perspective. He said, "I believe the message was that in the spirit of Apollo, a free and open spirit, you can attack a very difficult goal and achieve it if you can all agree on what the goal is."

Another five NASA missions made it to the moon between 1969 and 1972, and these days people wonder when we'll put a person on Mars. And of course I'd love to see that happen! But I'd also like to believe, as Armstrong did, that if we shoot for the stars we really can achieve our dreams here on planet Earth.

FANTASY 8397

CREEDENCE CLEARWATER REVIVAL

DUCK KEE MARKET
EER·WINE·FROZEN FOOD·PRODUCE·MEAT

TON'S

WILLY AND THE POOR BOYS

CREEDENCE CLEARWATER REVIVAL

While British Invasion bands were mining the blues for inspiration, Creedence Clearwater Revival dug deeper into the roots of American music, finding a rich vein of gold in the stomps and boogies of Cajun country. The California-bred foursome started playing local dances in their teens as the Blue Velvets, and included brothers Tom and John Fogerty. CCR's first hit was their feedback-dripping cover of Dale Hawkins' rockabilly classic "Suzie Q." Between 1968 and 1971, the band made six great albums of plainspoken, powerful American rock, including such timeless songs as "Proud Mary," the anti-war "Who'll Stop the Rain?" and the lacerating "Fortunate Son."

MARCHING AGAINST THE WAR

Massive anti-war protest at the Capitol Building in Washington, DC

The movement to end US involvement in the Vietnam War gained momentum when thousands of college students marched through Times Square and San Francisco in protest in 1964. By the end of 1968, American casualties in southeast Asia had surpassed all projections. There seemed to be no end in sight, and most public opinion polls showed that a majority of Americans were opposed to the war. On October 15, 1969, millions of Americans left jobs and schools to participate in local demonstrations around the country for the Moratorium to End the War in Vietnam. And on November 15, some half a million people marched against the war in Washington, DC. President Lyndon Johnson finally succumbed to the pressure and initiated the Paris Peace Negotiations with Vietnam.

The British band Led Zeppelin came thundering on the scene like some kind of Godzilla from across the ocean, with guitarist Jimmy Page breathing fire through his electric guitar and drummer John Bonham pounding on his kick drum loud enough to make your heart skip a beat. The Rolling Stones kicked off their 1969 release *Let It Bleed* with "Gimme Shelter," which was a legitimately frightening song about the fear of an increasingly violent world. That same year, four youths from Birmingham, England, formed a band and began exploring even darker corners of music and the mind. Black Sabbath, who debuted the following year, gave a name to doom and gloom—and scared the bejeezus out of listeners young and old.

In bands like Zeppelin and Sabbath were the underpinnings of heavy metal, a new breed of hard rock that took volume and power to new extremes. With the exception of a few fellow paint-peelers like Blue Cheer and Grand Funk Railroad, most rock & roll recordings prior to their appearance had a radio-friendly emphasis on the "high end"; that is, the upper, treble frequencies

While music can have a peaceful, healing effect, it can also be an outlet for anger.

that translated well through the small speakers on portable radios. But now the sound was getting big and boomy: heavily weighted on the low end as if rock itself was changing from the bottom up. *Join me or get out of my way*, it roared. Heavy metal represented all the pent-up anger and aggravation that had been building for years. And it angered and aggravated a lot of listeners! But that was the point, or at least part of it.

Music is a big waterfall. You can either ride with it or be pushed under. While music can have a peaceful, healing effect,

Crosby, Stills, Nash & Young

The gorgeous and complex vocal chemistry of David Crosby, Stephen Stills, Graham Nash, and Neil Young coalesced in 1969, and CSNY was born, just in time to play its second gig—at Woodstock. In 1970, their *Déjà Vu* album generated three hit singles: "Teach Your Children," "Our House," and the quartet's cover of Joni Mitchell's "Woodstock." Horrified by the shootings just weeks later at Kent State University (see page 260), Young wrote the moving and angry "Ohio." CSNY quickly recorded Young's direct challenge to the Nixon administration and rushed "Ohio" to radio. Even though it was widely banned, the song could not be repressed. "Ohio" became the expression of a generation's condemnation of government and their determination to put an end to the Vietnam War.

The youth movement was a tsunami, and the older generation could see the waters rising.

it can also be an outlet for anger. When it became clear that the status quo wasn't going to be brought down by the pea-shooters of happy-go-lucky Top 40 hits, a cadre of musicians, including the heavy metal players, armed themselves with more substantial weaponry.

The thirst for new means of expression led to extreme sounds. Outpourings of frustration with the establishment—including the established margins of what was acceptable in music—were taken to an even further extent in 1969 by two particularly notable bands. The Motor City Five, better known as MC5, and the Stooges, led by Iggy Pop, released their debuts that year, and in doing so launched the first full-fledged generation of punk music.

If rock was the anti-establishment sound, punk was the *anti-anti* sound, and it made no concessions to the technique or form of the music that preceded it. Punk scared off plenty of people—and heaven knows you weren't going to hear a note of it on your Cousin Brucie show—but you had to give these guys credit for being so dedicated to their cause and their music. There was no room to be phony. These punks got onstage and let fly every raw, primitive feeling bottled up inside. It must have been very therapeutic. I can't imagine that anyone who could belt out "Search and Destroy" would need to explore their inner feelings with a psychologist. I must admit, though, that whenever I listened to these records on my own, I needed to lie down afterward on somebody's couch.

In the Garden of Good
Though not always as extreme a form as heavy metal or punk, the countercultural

derground Newspapers

most widely circulated radical derground newspaper of the 60s was the *Los Angeles Free* hich cost 25 cents—"free" to the spirit of the paper's not its price! "The Freep" on the anti-war movement, the trial of the Chicago Seven, viewed Allen Ginsberg, Bob ack Panther leaders, and other counterculture touchstones. The *East Village Other* took up the charge in New York City, as did the *NOLA Express* in New Orleans. The underground press also exposed writers like Charles Bukowski, cartoonists like Robert Crumb, and introduced music fans to bands like Pink Floyd and the Pink Fairies. In response, the FBI started its own phony underground papers.

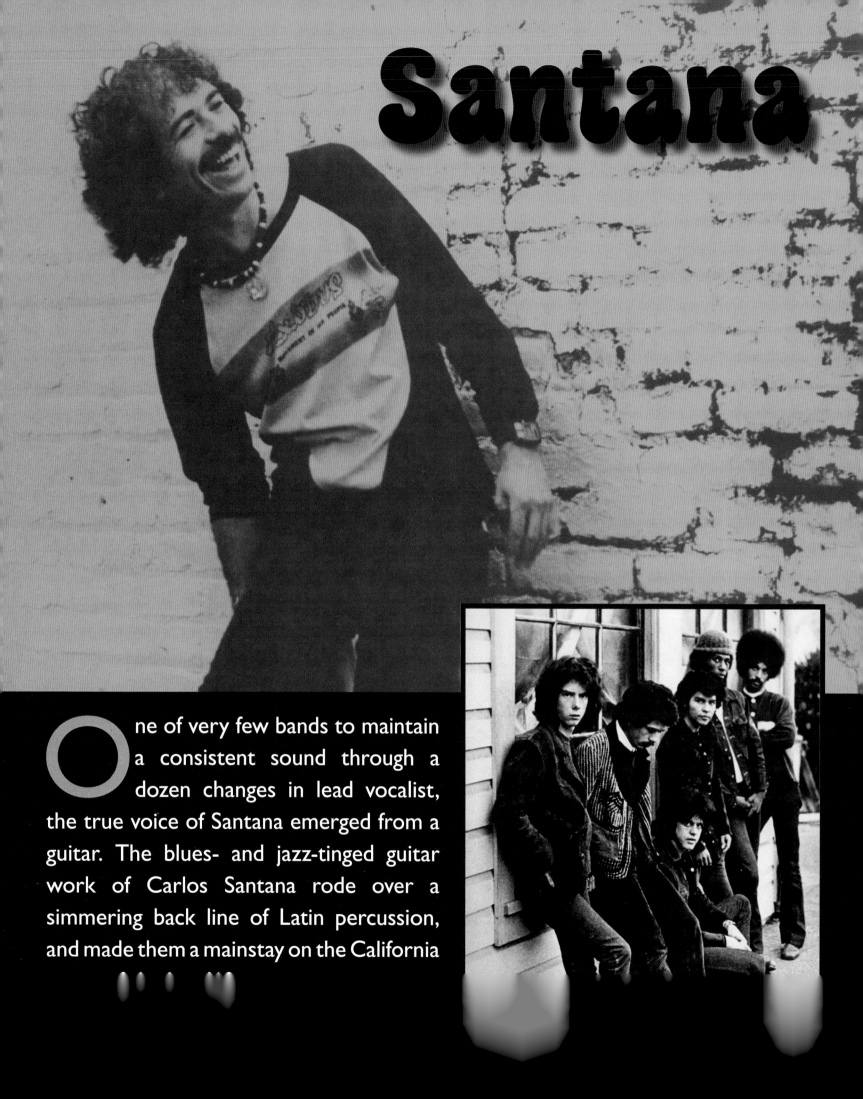

Santana

One of very few bands to maintain a consistent sound through a dozen changes in lead vocalist, the true voice of Santana emerged from a guitar. The blues- and jazz-tinged guitar work of Carlos Santana rode over a simmering back line of Latin percussion, and made them a mainstay on the California

movement of the 1960s dominated and defined the era. However, at the time, all those opposed to the momentous societal changes were determined to keep the voice of youth quiet. They knew there was a swell of resistance— there was no denying it—but they had hoped to prevent it from bringing on a wave of change. Boy, would they learn the hard way that they were wrong.

As the movement came to a head in 1969, it proved to be far more than a passing wave. The youth movement was a tsunami, and the older generation could see the waters rising on those occasions when young people gathered by the thousands. There were sit-ins, marches, peace rallies…and then, there was Woodstock.

A handful of music festivals had already been drawing crowds of alarming proportions when four east coast businessmen recognized a large-scale outdoor event could be a major money-maker. After being turned down by a number of small towns in rural New York, a gentle-hearted dairy farmer named Max Yasgur gave the promoters permission to use his land (reportedly, at the urging of his young son) in the

BLACK SABBATH

The dark lords of metal hailed from Birmingham, England, a decaying industrial city whose imposing gloom and factory din were mirrored in the band's threatening guitars and thudding drums. Black Sabbath debuted in 1970, fronted by the haunting vocals of Ozzy Osbourne, who has always seemed quite pleased and proud of his reputation as a very strange person.

THE CONCORDE

The world got a little smaller in 1969 with the inaugural flight of the Concorde. The SST (short for supersonic transport) turbojet could cross the Atlantic in half the time of a commercial airliner—and at twice the altitude. A passenger looking out a window on the Concorde could see stars in the daytime sky above and the curvature of the Earth below.

I'm a big fan of aviation, and twice had the pleasure of flying on the Concorde. A joint venture of Aérospatiale (doing business as Air France) and the British Aircraft Corporation, the Concorde flew just a few overseas routes from London and France to New York and Washington, DC. It had one narrow cabin, as if we were all in First Class, and despite the incredible speeds and the elevation above the jet stream, it provided the most peaceful, comfortable ride you can imagine. I never even had the sense of speed except on take off and landing. Even though we were breaking the speed of sound, passengers never heard that sonic boom; they heard it on the ground, but we were too far past it in the air. I remember that a meter mounted to the bulkhead displayed the current mach speed, and a voice would announce in a wonderful British baritone, "We are now traveling at mach 2.2. . . ."

Unfortunately, the small fleet of 20 Concordes was so obscenely expensive to build and maintain that it just couldn't survive in the airline industry. In the

words of Najeeb Halaby, then CEO and chairman of Pan Am, "Never have so few been flown for so much." It was officially grounded in 2003, not long after the tragic crash of Flight 4590 in Paris, which was caused by debris on the runway.

Near my home in New York City, a grounded Concorde sits on the deck of the Intrepid Sea, Air & Space Museum. It saddens me to see this magnificent aircraft being gawked at on a pier along the Hudson River. It looks to me like a bird chained to the ground.

The Guess Who

Canada has never exported a ton of rock & roll to the US, but these boys from Manitoba were a big hit on both sides of the border.

Sometimes tender and sometimes tough, the Guess Who's early hits included "These Eyes," "No Time," and "American Woman."

R&B IS ALL ABOUT THE EVERYDAY ADVENTURES OF THE HUMAN SPIRIT.

town of Bethel. According to legend, Yasgur cut a tongue-in-cheek deal with one of the young promoters: If anything went wrong, Yasgur would give him a crew cut. If everything went according to plan, the fifty-year-old farmer would let his own hair grow long.

Assuming he kept his word, ol' Max must have grown his hair down to his ankles. Smack dab in the middle of a violent, war-torn age, the Woodstock festival proved that huge numbers of people could come together in harmony and peace.

That's not to say *everything* went according to plan. The promoters said they expected no more than 50,000 ticketholders in a reasonably controlled,

three-day event from August 15–17, 1969. Even if they did have an inkling of how popular the show could become, they simply didn't understand what they had started. Within days of announcing the event, word spread like wildfire through the underground. The "Three Days of Peace & Music," as the promotional posters read, was destined to be transformed into an epicenter of the social revolution.

Soon almost every musician wanted to perform there, and the originally planned lineup of artists swelled in proportion to the half-million hippies headed to upstate New York. Folk artists on the roster included Richie Havens, Joan Baez, Tim Hardin, Country

The Jackson 5

Forged in the image of "schoolboy" doo wop groups like Frankie Lymon and the Teenagers, the Jackson brothers from Gary, Indiana, were the darlings of Motown Records in the early 1970s. Unlike the rest of the Motown roster, the dancin'-and-singin' Jacksons were produced with a young audience in mind; however, the sound was so infectious and the kids so incredibly talented that their appeal crossed barriers of age and race. No one before the Jacksons had their first four singles become number 1 songs; the quintet broke the mold with "I Want You Back," "ABC," "The Love You Save," and "I'll Be There." Front man—wait, let's make that front "kid"—Michael Jackson launched a solo career as a thirteen-year-old in 1971, breaking little girls' hearts with "Got to Be There."

Joe & the Fish, Arlo Guthrie, and crossovers Crosby, Stills, Nash & Young. Rock artists from across the spectrum constituted a Who's Who of the era's favorites: Santana, the Band, Creedence Clearwater Revival, Ten Years After, Joe Cocker, Jefferson Airplane, the Who, Sly & the Family Stone, the Grateful Dead, Janis Joplin, Blood, Sweat & Tears, Mountain, Jimi Hendrix…it would have taken three days just to name them all! And tucked right in among all of those happening hippie stars was the campy doo wop group Sha-Na-Na. Go figure.

Even when things started getting messy in the rain, the scene there on Yasgur's farm was a beautiful sight. As I wandered the grounds in my own kind of hippie haze, all I could think was that it was like a garden—a huge, swaying garden of flower children. Everyone was dressed in bright colors, and when their clothes came off there was a rainbow of dancing bodies. The nudity was never lascivious. It was just people being natural and unmasked. There were children playing in mud puddles and older people reviving their youth. We all forgot airplanes, telephones, and trains. If the festival had been held in current

Three Dog Night

Three Dog Night was named for an Australian expression: The colder the night in the outback, the more dogs you need to pile up with to keep warm. The band scored twenty-one hit singles and twelve consecutive gold albums from 1969 to 1975. Their biggest hits were covers: Hoyt Axton's "Joy to the World," Randy Newman's "Mama Told Me (Not to Come)," and Harry Nilsson's "One."

The Band

This Canadian folk-rock group brought rock & roll back to its roots. With skilled instrumentalism and a down-home authenticity, the Band scored big in 1968 with "The Weight" (from *Music from Big Pink*, named for the pink house in upstate New York where they recorded) and in 1969 with "The Night They Drove Old Dixie Down." They were also well known as the band that played behind Bob Dylan on his '66 world tour.

times, no one would even have brought a cellphone—plus, they'd be naked, so where would they keep it? (All right, none of that now.) It was back to basics, and that's what Woodstock was all about: returning to the fundamentals of who and what we are as a community of people. And for a few days, it worked.

Hip vs. Square

Another law of physics for you to consider: For every action, there is an equal and opposite reaction.

Woodstock was the grand total of the '60s and a remarkable representation of the Shangri-La imagined by a peace-loving generation. But to everyone who opposed their views, it was evidence of the chaotic and irresponsible nature of America's youth. It was an action that warranted an equal and opposite reaction.

Unfortunately, a huge portion of the media aligned itself with conservative naysayers, and Woodstock was widely reported as a crashing failure. "What a nightmare!" they cried. "There were no bathrooms, no food, no facilities! The police were powerless against the drugged-out mob of lowlife hippies!"

Communal Living

Hippies groove in the movie **The Love-Ins.**

Communes were truly living experiments—communities of people who shared not only housing but also possessions and food. Some communes formed around spiritual or political leaders, while others were comprised of people simply looking for a cheaper, more sociable way to live. Nudism and vegetarianism were popular in hippie communes—just two more alternative lifestyle choices that did a great job of freaking out the "straights." Some hippies went "back to the land," creating working farms in rural areas. A few of the more unusual communes made many wonder if there was a line between communes and cults, and on the darkest side of communal living, mind-altering drugs mixed with personality cults like Charles Manson's murderous "family."

The Stonewall Riots and the Birth of the Gay Rights Movement

Scene from the documentary
Before Stonewall: The Making of a Gay and Lesbian Community

During the 1960s, the American Psychiatric Association still listed homosexuality as a sociopathic personality disorder. People discovered to be gay were fired from jobs, thrown out of housing, jailed, and institutionalized. Anyone found to be gay was discharged from military service and could be prosecuted for sodomy.

Police clamped down on bars where gays congregated, like the Stonewall Inn in NYC's liberal Greenwich Village. When the Stonewall was raided on June 28, 1969, the patrons fought back and ten police officers had to barricade themselves inside the bar as an angry crowd gathered. Riots erupted for two nights as thousands of people demonstrated in the streets, demanding an end to the persecution of homosexuals. Within two years, there were gay activist groups in every major US city, and the Stonewall riots went down in history as the call to arms for the Gay Rights Movement.

People could believe a man had walked on the moon—they'd seen it that same summer with their own eyes. But they couldn't believe a bunch of hippies could get together without trouble.

Those of us who were there in Bethel knew there was no panic, no claustrophobia, no fear of a riot. The police weren't powerless—they just realized there was nothing to fear and joined in the fun. Bathrooms would have been nice, but we made do (so to speak). When we ran out of food, we shared. Anyone who has been with others during a blackout or surrounded by strangers when tragedy strikes knows that these kinds of situations bring out the best in human nature. Everybody helps everyone else out. It's too bad this doesn't happen more often, but Woodstock was one of those times.

Yet, for the other side, it was fodder for criticism and negativity. If any single musical moment from Woodstock captured the polarized response, it was when Jimi Hendrix performed his instrumental version of "The Star-Spangled Banner" early on the morning of August 18. Hendrix (who had himself volunteered for the US Army) painted

Woodstock was destined to be the epicenter of a generation.

a complete contemporary picture of the nation: His guitar lines expressed the soaring spirit of patriotism paired with the horrific squeal of bombs falling through the air. For the like-minded fans who absorbed his poetry, Hendrix's rendition was perfectly representative of the times. But for the mainstream, it was an abomination.

Central Scrutinizers

I don't want to sound too bleak about the contrast between young and old. We loved our parents and our grammies, and they loved us back. You could wear your hair down to your behind and still get a smile from the nice lady across the street. Many hands have always reached across from each side of the aisle. As

Neil Diamond

Neil Diamond has been making beautiful noise since he was a teenager in the late '50s. From his 1966 hit "Cherry, Cherry" and on through "Holly Holy," "Girl, You'll Be a Woman Soon," and "Sweet Caroline," he wove pure gold with little more than a three-chord progression on an acoustic guitar and a potent vocal delivery. In a career that preceded the golden age of rock & roll—and has endured long after—Neil proves that a well-crafted song will win over an audience regardless of passing trends and styles.

anyone who has listened to my radio show knows, I believe we're all cousins.

But it's usually the loudest voices that are heard and paid attention to, and in 1969 everyone on the far left and far right were screaming at each other. You don't get that kind of opposition unless each side believes it has good reason to be *fearful* of the other. For example, young people feared being drafted into a war they didn't believe in; and the US government feared a generation that was ready to burn their draft cards. They knew these kids weren't just some angry villagers at the gate. They had a genuine revolution on their hands.

Fear—some would say paranoia—on the part of the government led to some extraordinary measures. They actually took steps to deport cultural leaders like John Lennon, whom the establishment feared could provoke legions of fans with a speech or a song. Remember in 1966, when his quote that the Beatles were "more popular than Jesus" was taken out of context? It's as if people believed Lennon could singlehandedly end Christianity, and they started burning Beatles records by the truckload.

Radio stations, too, were starting

Counterculture on the Big screen

Dennis Hopper, Peter Fonda, and Jack Nicholson "head out on the highway" in Easy Rider.

Countercultural films like *Easy Rider* and *M*A*S*H* ushered in the "New Hollywood"—the major studios realized that hippies liked movies, too, and a long-hair dollar was just as valuable as any other. The 1969 road movie *Easy Rider* cost $375,000 to make and raked in $19 million at the box office. It made anti-establishment stars of Jack Nicholson, Dennis Hopper, and Peter Fonda, and turned Steppenwolf's "Born to Be Wild" into a monster rock hit. Concert films like *Woodstock* and the Rolling Stones documentary *Gimme Shelter* brought the era's greatest musical performances to movie audiences around the world. Meanwhile, sentiment against the Vietnam War fueled dark comedies like Robert Altman's *M*A*S*H*, *Catch-22*, and the gentler *Alice's Restaurant*, starring folksinger Arlo Guthrie.

to be censored by some very scared conservatives. They kept all kinds of songs off the air, particularly if a subtext about drugs was suspected. Over the years we would see some really ridiculous exclusions. I couldn't spin "Snowbird" by Anne Murray—Anne Murray!—because it was thought that "snow" was cocaine. And they pulled "Puff the Magic Dragon" because someone decided *Puff* was *draggin'* on a marijuana joint rolled by Little Jackie *Paper*. Sometimes you had to wonder who was smoking what. But my station programmers were obeying an edict that had come from the FCC, and the FCC was listening to congressmen, and the congressmen were likely listening to their wives.

Probably the greatest fear stems from apprehension of the unfamiliar. Musicians like Jimi Hendrix and Janis Joplin were totally foreign to the generation reared on Perry Como and Doris Day. Rock music separated the two camps much like drug use did: For young people it was a passage to euphoria; to their parents, it was emblematic of danger and loss of control. Sadly, Hendrix and Joplin both passed away of drug-related

Cousin Brucie's Top Anti-War Songs

"Fortunate Son"
Creedence Clearwater Revival

"Sky Pilot"
The Animals

"What Is Truth?"
Johnny Cash

"I Should Be Proud"
Martha and the Vandellas

"Ball of Confusion"
The Temptations

"Masters of War"
Bob Dylan

"Where Have All the Flowers Gone?"
Kingston Trio

"Bring Them Home"
Pete Seeger

"Volunteers"
Jefferson Airplane

"White Boots Marching in a Yellow Land"
Phil Ochs

"Feel-Like-I'm Fixin'-to-Die Rag"
Country Joe and the Fish

"Ohio"
Crosby, Stills, Nash & Young

"Give Peace a Chance"
John Lennon

causes in 1969. For their fans, it was sheer tragedy. For those who opposed everything those artists stood for, it was a morose kind of validation.

Diamonds in the Rough

To this day, we tend to take the easy route by deciding someone is unlike us before seeing the many ways in which we are the same. But there are always the moderates, and they are the reasonable, open-minded people who walk a line between two well-defined sides.

Several musicians were appealing to young and old audiences simultaneously. To my ears, artists like Neil Sedaka, Dion, Paul Anka, Frankie Avalon, Bobby Rydell, Freddy Cannon, Jay & the Americans, and Connie Francis have all been sold a bit short by rock & roll fans. The great songwriter Doc Pomus shouldn't be forgotten, either: He penned the lyrics to classics like "A Teenager in Love" (Dion and the Belmonts), "This Magic Moment" and "Save the Last Dance For Me" (both for Ben E. King and the Drifters). And how about Neil Diamond? There were few hits on the radio that rivaled "Solitary Man," "Cherry, Cherry," "Cracklin' Rosie" or "Kentucky Woman."

Neil was destined for superstardom but came across like the everyday guy you could relate to, a mantle later picked up by Bruce Springsteen in the 1970s. Like many of the other artists named above, Neil Diamond's songs had all the markings of rock & roll: passionate, rhythmically driven, and catchy as all get-out. And I swear, this isn't just one Brooklyn boy patting another one on the back!

I'll tell you why else I think these artists are important to the times we've been remembering here. They represented common ground. In their songs we could erase the line between generations, even if for just for three and a half minutes. Aside from those rare musical moments, the generations in America were living separate lives. At the end of the decade we stood shell shocked by all the change, all the pain, and all the intense conflict witnessed over ten years' time. Music provided one way to heal the wound, or at least make it feel better for a while.

The crack in the pavement that had separated young and old early in the decade had, by 1969, become a canyon. The two generations couldn't even yell to one another from across the gap. We just could not hear one another anymore.

Jeff Beck

Jeff Beck is a guitarist's guitarist—relentlessly innovative and trend-setting. His playing in the Yardbirds and the Jeff Beck Group consistently broke new ground. Much of his recorded work has been instrumental, and has ranged from blues-rock to metal and fusion.

Blood, Sweat & Tears

With a big ensemble and an eclectic sound, BS&T fused rock, pop, blues, and jazz. The band was led by keyboardist Al Kooper, a top-shelf session musician who had played with legends including Bob Dylan, Jimi Hendrix, and the Who. An industry icon in his own right, Kooper was also fundamental to the careers of the Zombies and Lynyrd Skynyrd.

Janis Joplin

Rod Stewart

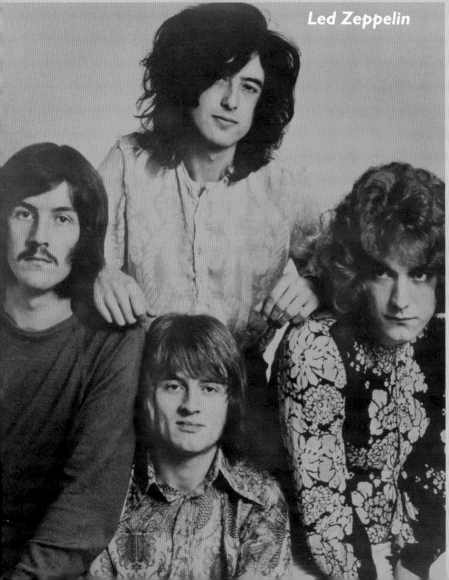
Led Zeppelin

Elton John

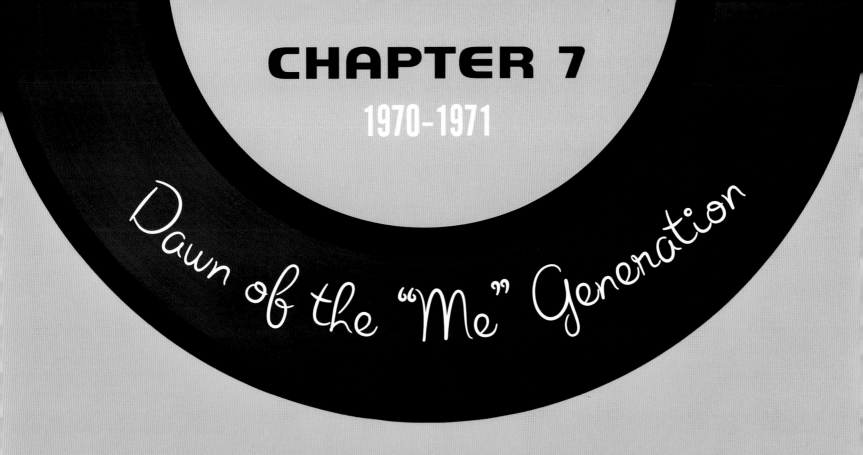

CHAPTER 7

1970-1971

Dawn of the "Me" Generation

There's an expression that says hindsight is 20/20, but I believe time can also cause things to go out of focus. Many of us have idealized hippie life and made bad guys out of "the establishment" of the '60s. In truth, though, there were plenty of long-haired kids who were complete knuckleheads and just as many suit-and-tie types who were a heck of a lot of fun at parties. Things are never so black and white.

Gazing over our own history, we also tend to draw bold lines between the decades, as if the '50s were all sock hops and crew cuts and the '60s were a drugged-out free-for-all. But it's not as if we woke up on January 1, 1970, wearing bell bottoms and a smiley-face tee shirt. There was no New Year's change, but rather, a soft cross-dissolve between the '60s and '70s.

Cool Out

As we took stock of our wins and losses, the fires of revolution were starting to cool. The '60s had been such a volatile decade that continuing at the same pace was just too much for anyone to take. Once we started to mellow out, to take a breather from the battle, our music started to soften around the

The '60s had been such a volatile decade that continuing at the same pace was just too much for anyone to take.

edges as well. In the early '70s, a wave of peaceful, soothing songs washed over the airwaves, and it has proven to be some of the most beloved music of our time.

Elton John waded into the mainstream with "Your Song," the lovely opening track of his self-titled record from 1970. Cat Stevens released *Tea for the Tillerman*, arguably his finest moment, and had hits with "Wild World" and the touching "Father and Son." During the same period, listeners fell for the Carpenters ("Close to You"), Bread ("Make It with You"), and the lovely wonder from down under, Olivia Newton-John ("If Not For You"). James Taylor—embodiment of the sensitive singer-songwriter—fingerpicked his way

into our hearts with "You've Got a Friend" and "Fire and Rain." Taylor had recently overcome personal struggles when he had his commercial breakthrough, and the autobiographical "Fire and Rain" seemed to represent the whole generation's shift from tough times to post-'60s peace of mind.

All of these tunes were tagged as "soft rock"—something of an oxymoron, you might say, but the phrase was fitting for a style that smoothed the hard edges of music that had come before. It was to music what impressionism is to art: a meticulously created style with all of the meticulous details kind of blurred.

Even artists with a rocking history started to roll with the changes. Elvis had a huge hit with "The Wonder of

The Beatles Break Up

In April 1970, Paul McCartney released his first solo album, *McCartney*. Several days later he announced that he was leaving the Beatles. Within a month, the Beatles' *Let It Be* album was released—a later documentary of the making of the album gave devastated fans some insight into the tension that had built up between band members. The Beatles did not publicly confirm their breakup, though, until December 31, 1970, when Paul filed a lawsuit against John, George, and Ringo in order to dissolve the band (Happy New Year, kids).

For years, fans hoped for a reunion that never came. It was sad to see them go, but in retrospect maybe it was time for these four hugely talented artists to follow their individual muses. Without ever resting on laurels—and those were some laurels!—each member of the Beatles went on to explore the depth of his creativity in a successful solo career.

ELTON JOHN

In an era of guitar-driven rock & roll, pop pianist Elton John (born Reginald Kenneth Dwight) managed to dominate rock radio in the mid 1970s. His outsized stage costumes—and a very curious collection of eyeglasses—belied the fact that Elton was actually quite shy. In one of the most seamless and successful collaborations in rock & roll, Elton put music and voice to the legendary lyrics of Bernie Taupin. Their combined talent yielded some of the prettiest, most singable hits on record, including the 1970 breakthrough hit "Your Song," "Daniel," "Rocket Man," and "Don't Let the Sun Go Down on Me." All seven albums he released between 1972 and 1975 went straight to number 1. Elton, by the way, was also a good friend of John Lennon—so good he was named godfather of John's son Sean.

BREAD

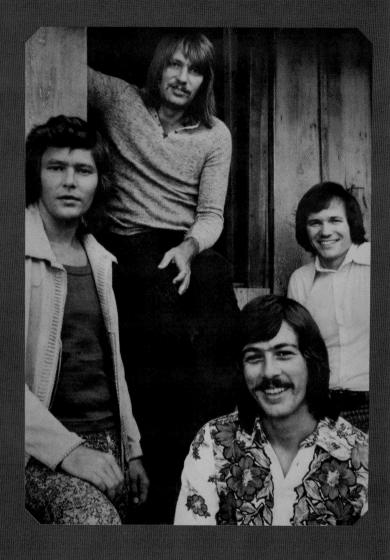

A pop band from Los Angeles, Bread found commercial success in the '70s with singles like "Make It with You" and "The Guitar Man." Their melodical, easygoing sound came to epitomize soft rock.

You," Rod Stewart had a great love song in "Maggie May," and the Rolling Stones tamed their sound for "Wild Horses." The blaring horns of Chicago were quieted for "Colour My World," and Derek & the Dominos, featuring guitarists Eric Clapton and Duane Allman, cooled down with "Bell Bottom Blues."

Soft rock was not just a genre, but a songwriting craft. The ultimate example—and one of the most successful records in pop history—is Carole King's *Tapestry*. It's a very special album and has always stayed with me. I remember playing cuts like "It's Too Late," "I Feel the Earth Move," and "Will You Love Me Tomorrow?" on my radio show years ago, and hearing those songs today is like listening to old friends speak. Each of the cuts on Carole's album is like a new road to travel on. Especially when I hear "So Far Away," I feel like I'm taking a romantic musical journey. By the way, cousins, *Tapestry* stayed on the charts for *six years*, ranking for a time as the best-selling record of all time, and has sold over 10 million copies in the US alone. That means there's a copy of Carole's album in one of every six or seven households in the country!

From *We* to *Me*

Could it be that Americans had learned so much from the turbulent '60s that now we were easing off? To look at the song charts, the early '70s seemed to be a time of increasing calm and reflection. We weren't yet ready to let go of our idealism entirely, but we were maturing and gaining new priorities. Older brothers and sisters were starting families, moving from the cities to the suburbs, and getting on with the next phase of life. Whether we were frustrated at not being able to break the system—or felt we had done our job setting changes in motion—much of the energy that had been spent on bettering the world now seemed to be directed inward.

A new era of personal enrichment was taking hold. Concepts of self-awareness, self-help, and self-improvement started to take over the national conscience. I don't believe that we were becoming selfish, necessarily, but people seemed to be thinking they stood a better chance of making headway with their inner world than with the world at large. "Respect Yourself," the Staple Singers told us. A shift began that turned us from the "we" generation into the "me" generation.

Delaney & Bonnie

The earthy and bluesy husband-and-wife duo Delaney and Bonnie Bramlett went largely unappreciated in their time; their biggest song in the US was "Never Ending Song of Love" from 1970. But they sure kept good company, and among fellow musicians they garnered a great deal of respect. D&B shared concert bills with the likes of Blind Faith and John Lennon's Plastic Ono band, and they had a big influence on peers like Eric Clapton, Duane Allman, and George Harrison. In fact, Delaney reportedly showed George how to play slide guitar, a signature of his solo-era sound.

JANIS JOPLIN

Gritty, bluesy, and passionate, Janis Joplin gave a little piece of her heart to every song she sang. Her vocal swagger made this Texas singer the queen bee of San Francisco's psychedelic rock scene, where she fronted blues-rockers Big Brother and the Holding Company.

Joplin's solo album, *Pearl*, was released in 1971, shortly after her death at age 27 of a heroin overdose. *Pearl* held the number 1 spot for nine weeks in 1971, thanks in large part to her most popular song, "Me and Bobby McGee," written by Kris Kristofferson and Fred Rogers.

The First Earth Day

Birth of the Environmental Movement

On April 22, 1970, twenty million Americans demonstrated against the destruction of the environment in rallies around the country. This first Earth Day was the brainchild of Wisconsin Senator Gaylord Nelson, who called it "an environmental teach-in." Pete Seeger performed at the Washington, DC rally, and Paul Newman and Ali McGraw were at the New York City event. Soon after, Congress passed the Clean Air Act and created the United States Environmental Protection Agency. Today, Earth Day is observed in 175 countries and is celebrated by a half billion people each year.

Because April 22nd is the birthday of Vladimir Lenin, the Russian revolutionary, conservatives accused Nelson of being a commie. He responded: "A person many consider the world's first environmentalist, Saint Francis of Assisi, was born on April 22. More importantly, so was my Aunt Tillie."

That's what the easygoing soft rock music was all about. With lifestyle changes came a taste for a different kind of song and a pensive lyric.

Artists like Simon and Garfunkel, the Hollies, and Van Morrison flourished as listeners became attuned to more refined, sweet sounds. Maybe, with these songs ringing pleasantly in the background, we could free our minds without banging our heads against the wall.

I have always believed that the longstanding appeal of this music is that it provides comfort. It's so warm and relaxed. There was no getting comfortable in the '60s. We were too busy, we had serious repairs to make, we had a righteous agenda. But it was exhausting! After stomping our feet for ten years straight, it was time to lean back into a comfortable cushion.

Hard Truth

Before we could ever get too comfortable, though, the real world kept crashing back in on us. While the '70s are remembered today as "the 'me' decade," we could never disappear completely into our own private worlds. Not when student demonstrators were being shot dead on the campus of Kent State University (see page 260). Not when we had a president who promised to end the Vietnam War but instead escalated the fighting. And not when that same president confirmed our distrust in authority by deceiving us with the Watergate scandal.

Our disillusionment was all the more painful because there had been so much great headway, with many of the ideals we'd fought for in the '60s being integrated into the mainstream. The struggle for equal rights had led to a full-blown women's movement. Newfound sexual liberation was evident in racy books, television shows, and movies. Widespread desegregation resulted from the Civil Rights Movement. But we had spilled a lot of blood, sweat, and tears to get where we were, only to be left disappointed and still badly in need of answers. The Moody Blues summed it up well in the opening lines of their hit "Question" from *A Question of Balance*:

Why do we never get an answer
When we're knocking at the door
With a thousand million questions
About hate and death and war?

JOHN DENVER

John Denver's sunny country pop expressed his true reverence for America's natural beauty. He broke through in 1971 with "Take Me Home, Country Roads." His 1973 hit "Rocky Mountain High" became an official Colorado state song—despite the fact that uptight radio programmers often banned it, having misread John's lyric as an ode to getting high by less natural means. Gimme a break—John's song was no more about weed than was "Puff the Magic Dragon."

Edwards brought an edgy, electric sound to folk music, which enabled him to take protest-style folk songs into the mainstream. He hit it big with crossover singles like "Sunshine" and "Shanty."

THE PARTRIDGE FAMILY

A fictional family band with a laundry list of real-life hits, the Partridge Family was the subject of a '70s TV series featuring heartthrob David Cassidy as singer Keith Partridge. *The Partridge Family* show, based loosely on the Cowsills family of the '60s, documented the ups and downs of stardom. Supported on recordings by session musicians, the Partridge Family's singles included "I Think I Love You" and "I'll Meet You Halfway."

Neil Young

A Canadian artist who embraced distinctly American music traditions, Neil Young has been a constant in the evolution of folk rock. Known for his soul-searching lyrics and distinctive tenor vocals, Young recorded and performed solo as well as in bands like Buffalo Springfield and Crosby, Stills, Nash & Young. "Heart of Gold" and "Old Man" are two of the most beloved pieces from his solo career.

The Carpenters

Siblings Karen and Richard Carpenter were the poster children of '70s soft rock. Songs like "(They Long to Be) Close to You" and "We've Only Just Begun" featured Karen's honeyed alto buttressed by Richard's stately piano playing and meticulous arrangements. Karen is remembered for that sleepy, silky voice, but few people know she's also heard on Carpenters hits as the duo's drummer. Fewer still know that she was a terrific softball pitcher. I have personal experience on this one. She struck me out three times!

At the same time that listeners were getting all cozy with the soft rock sound, a lot of rock & roll artists were asking these kinds of questions—and not always in the polite way that the Moodies did. The Who vowed to keep fightin' the good fight in "Won't Get Fooled Again," and artists such as the Guess Who (no relation!), the Rolling Stones, and Led Zeppelin showed there was still plenty of fuel left in the hard rock tank.

Heavy-hitting bands were selling records by the hundreds of thousands, yet they didn't send as many hit singles up the mainstream charts as their soft rock brothers did. Instead, hard rock groups started to become the darlings of FM radio. On that side of the dial, the seeds of "album-oriented rock"—AOR, for short—were being planted. AOR deejays dug the extended jams and "concept album" cuts favored by the likes of Santana, Traffic, Jethro Tull, and the Band, and their programming would become the format of choice for hard rock in the mid 1970s. So, while your Cousin Brucie and fellow AM colleagues were plugging away with reliable, two-and-a-half-minute hits from the soft rock and R&B crowd, the distorted guitars

Joan Baez

Well known for her folk covers like "The Night They Drove Old Dixie Down" (originally by the Band), Baez is also remembered for her romantic and professional connection with a young Bob Dylan. She would document this strained relationship on the hit single "Diamonds and Rust."

KENT STATE

Protesting against the Vietnam War was commonplace across the country.

Fear and violence—it's truly a toxic combination. I think you can trace just about everything bad that's ever happened between humans on this planet to fear and violence. On May 4, 1970, the two collided on the campus of Kent State University, making for one of the darkest days in America's long, proud history.

The sad irony behind the shootings at Kent State University is that they resulted from one layer upon another of people trying to bring violence to a stop. The students were demonstrating against the violence in Vietnam, which had appeared to be tapering off until news came that President Nixon and company had decided to invade Cambodia. The Ohio National Guard was called out of fear that the students were going to become violent and destructive. Why these "weekend warriors" were even issued live rounds of ammunition still baffles me. And while no one knows exactly why the Guardsmen started firing on students, the two options are that they either feared what the students stood for or feared for their own safety.

The whole mess was never really sorted out. Students had been provocative and even burned down the ROTC building on campus, the Governor and local officials were panicked, and the Ohio National Guard itself was inexperienced. All in all, it was another lethal combination. In the end, four students lay dead and another nine injured, including one who was permanently paralyzed. In case you need more evidence that violence solves nothing, the attempt to silence students led immediately to a nationwide student strike that forced the closing of several hundred colleges and universities.

The impact was profound and long-lasting. H. R. Haldeman, President Nixon's chief of staff and a convicted architect of Watergate, wrote in his memoir *The Ends Of Power* that, "Kent State marked the beginning of Nixon's downhill slide toward Watergate." Unfortunately, it seems we have to get that low and mired in the mud before real change can happen. But the scope of Kent State's impact got so big, so fast, that it was easy to lose sight of the actual lives lost. I try never to forget that they were four normal kids who might just as easily been spending the afternoon at a concert as at a protest. Their names: Jeffrey Miller, Allison Krause, William Schroeder, and Sandra Scheuer.

Recently I received a letter from a listener. He had just visited Ohio and, being near the Kent State campus, had the events of May 1970 ringing in his mind. When he saw a middle-aged woman wearing a Kent State sweatshirt at a ballgame, he felt compelled to go talk to her. Had she been at Kent State on that fateful day in 1970?

As it turned out, she had. She was a freshman at the time, and recalled for him a day of anger, fear, violence, and sadness.

These two Americans—one having lived at the epicenter of an historical event, the other only having read about it—shared a moment of brotherhood and sympathy together. They took stock of where we were then and where we are now, forty years later. To me, that letter is a testimony to how deeply the Kent State shootings cut our nation. The wound is healed now, but the scars will always remain.

Led Zeppelin

Mystical, primal, and heavier than any band before them, Led Zeppelin heralded a new level of artistry and power in rock music. In sound and image, this British quartet stamped out a model for hard rock that countless bands tried hard to follow. While they are often regarded as the ultimate heavy metal band, many miss the fact that their album-oriented rock is deeply steeped in the blues—even if they did give the style a good pounding. Their eight-minute epic "Stairway to Heaven," never released as a single, remains one of radio's all-time most-requested rock songs.

James Taylor

Sweet *Baby James* (1970) introduced James Taylor's gentle singing and pristine acoustic fingerpicking, ushering in the singer-songwriter era with hits like "Fire and Rain" and "Country Road." Taylor's cover of Carole King's "You've Got a Friend" won Grammys in 1971 for both Taylor (Best Pop Vocal Performance, Male) and King (Song of the Year).

and battle-ready drumbeats of hard rock had their own home on the FM dial.

FM had established a distinct format by 1971, but its programmers were also ready to adopt some of the earmarks (pardon the pun) of good ol' Top 40 AM radio. You can still hear it today on terrestrial FM with the unending stream of jingles and promos, the loss of the long cut, and of course the inclusion of commercials. *We now interrupt these commercials to play a record!*

There was no hiding from the commercialism of rock & roll radio. The youth movement had by now become so huge and undeniable that young audiences were just ripe for the pickin'. Even underground radio, which had evolved from university stations transmitting revolutionary ideas and revolutionary music, was unearthed and forced up into the light as the pressure to cash in mounted on every side.

Whether they were spun on AM or FM, though, records of the day were benefitting from a giant leap in sonic fidelity. In recording studios, artists and producers were getting particular about audio quality, and they started applying techniques and high-end equipment that had only been used before on classical and jazz records. Album tracks had new depth and dimension, and when you listened with headphones on, the sound was incredible. It was like you were sitting in a concert hall, except that no one else was there to spill beer on you or dance on your foot.

That very personal experience with music—not just listening to it, but getting totally lost in it—played well at a time when people were taking all sorts of inner journeys. It wouldn't have been possible had audio technology not been steadily improving for years, though there certainly were failures along the way. One of the worst of the lot was what we called *quadraphonic sound*. At a time when fans were starting to spend a lot of money on expensive stereo components, it seemed like a great idea to deliver four separate channels of audio on a record so that listeners could surround themselves with speakers on every side (and this was the precursor to the surround-sound technology so popular today). If two-channel stereo was good, wouldn't four channels be twice as cool? But "quad" never sounded as good as planned, the record companies

Yes

Breaking through to FM radio was no easy trick for Yes, the granddaddies of progressive rock. Virtuosic performances, adventuresome orchestrations, and compositions of epic length would have kept a lesser band off the airwaves forever, but this Birmingham group crossed over to the mainstream in 1972 with the AOR hit "Roundabout."

Early 1970s TV

Jean Stapleton, Sally Struthers, Carroll O'Connor, and Rob Reiner in **All in the Family**

By the 1970s, our love affair with the television was riding high. Cable TV and recordable video did not arrive till later in the decade, so we watched what the prime time networks scheduled. We didn't know any better, but much of it was pretty good.

When *All in the Family* arrived in 1971, it immediately became the show everyone had to watch. It also changed situation comedies forever. Working class couple Archie and Edith Bunker, brilliantly portrayed by Carroll O'Connor and Jean Stapleton, were not the Cleavers of the 1950s. Archie's prejudices knew no boundaries, and his verbal sparring with liberal son-in-law, Mike "Meathead" Stivic, played by

Rob Reiner, mirrored the social and political commentary of the times. Sally Struthers rounded out the cast as Archie and Edith's daughter, Gloria.

Though light years from the battling Bunkers, *The Partridge Family*, about a squeaky clean show-biz family starring Shirley Jones and David Cassidy, was an instant hit. It didn't hurt that Cassidy quickly became the teen idol of the moment. Meanwhile, husband and wife crooners Sonny and Cher Bono had a surprise hit with a variety show aptly called *The Sonny & Cher Comedy Hour*, while Flip Wilson, as alter ego Geraldine, insisted that, "the devil made me do it," on *The Flip Wilson Show*.

Mary Tyler Moore also started her long run as a charming Minneapolis career gal in *The Mary Tyler Moore Show*, while Lucille Ball was still making us laugh in *Here's Lucy*. Speaking of laughter, Redd Foxx and Demond Wilson took the "junk" business to a new level in *Sanford & Son*, while truly odd couple Tony Randall and Jack Klugman played off each other perfectly in *The Odd Couple*.

Alan Alda (third from left) heads the cast of M*A*S*H.

Peter Falk as Lt. Columbo

We were also introduced to one of television's most iconic detectives, *Columbo*, played by the brilliant Peter Falk. Dogging each episode's guest murderer in his rumpled raincoat and with his understated wit, Columbo always solved the case, but not before driving his adversary crazy by asking, "Just one more thing...." *Kojak* starred Telly Savalas as a hard-bitten New York City detective fond of saying "Who loves ya, baby?" while Robert Young and James Brolin made us feel comfortable in the waiting room—no mean feat—on one of the most popular doctor shows ever, *Marcus Welby, M.D.*

M*A*S*H was a hit show about the ups and downs of an army hospital during the Korean War and had a terrific ensemble cast led by Alan Alda. It took great joy in pointing out the folly of war—maybe that's why we liked it so much. Meanwhile, James Arness, in the classic western *Gunsmoke* rode his twentieth and final season into the sunset.

Later in the decade, when cable television and a magical recording device called the VCR took hold, television would reinvent itself again, and we were given the opportunity to change the way we select, record, and watch entertainment on "the box" from then on.

PING-PONG INITIATES US-CHINA RELATIONS

The Great Wall of China

The Cold War had chilled relations between the United States and Communist China to a deep freeze, when a chance encounter between two Ping-Pong players led to a thaw. American champ Glenn Cowan missed his team's bus one day while the US Table Tennis team was competing in Japan. A Chinese player waved him onto the Chinese bus. Cowan stepped off the bus with one of the Chinese players into a swarm of photographers, and the US team received an invitation from Chairman Mao Zedong to play in China soon after. On April 12, 1971, the US team became the first American sports delegation to enter the Chinese capital since 1949. Mao Zedong's "Ping-Pong diplomacy" paved the way for President Nixon's historic visit to China in February 1972.

The Osmonds

This All-American family band got its start singing in barbershops in their native Utah. With devout Mormon ideals and a wholesome image, the group exploded onto the pop scene in 1971 with "One Bad Apple." The Osmonds' long string of hits helped catapult youngest siblings Donny and Marie onto further success as the co-hosts of their squeaky-clean variety show on television. They're both still among the nicest people in the whole industry. In September 2006, Donny began a run as Gaston in the Broadway production of *Beauty and the Beast*.

didn't embrace it, and only a handful of big commercial records were ever released in the format. Quadraphonic technology was a clunker. It's kind of like the Edsel of the audio industry.

Cousins, I have to make a confession here. I fell prey to the audio industry's hype and purchased a quad unit of my own. Another confession: I'm still trying to figure out how convert this thing into a toaster.

Signs, Signs, Everywhere Signs

Rock & roll continued to splinter both stylistically and in terms of the messages sent. Depending on the groove and the lyrics, a song could tell you to rock out, to chill out, to make out, or to get out. Canadian rockers Five Man Electrical Band were still toeing the line when they sang "Signs" (*Do this, don't do that / can't you read the sign?*), but the less oppositional message of the flower children—peace!—was coming back around in a refreshing new way.

Peace became a running theme on records of the early 1970s, and in them you could hear earnest calls to cut the tension between lovers, brothers, and countries. Just a few of the many examples include great tunes like "All Right Now" (Free), "Who'll Stop the Rain" (CCR), "Revival (Love Is Everywhere)" (Allman Bros.), "Joy to the World" (Three Dog Night), and "Peace Train" (Cat Stevens). It may sound a little corny now, but you couldn't listen to songs like those without picturing yourself holding hands with a bunch of friends in some sunny, flowered field. Long before the MTV era, these songs played like video imagery in my mind.

The pinnacle of peace music has to be John Lennon's "Imagine," the gentle piano ballad from his 1971 solo album of the same name. It was one of the first times people in the Western world heard this incredible suggestion: Throw away all of your possessions, they're meaningless. Throw away all of your preconceptions, your biases, your politics and religion, and just imagine a world living in peace. Lennon had been a leader of the peace movement, but never before had he or anyone else expressed what this planet needed so simply or beautifully. "Imagine" still has the power today that it did back then. And we've yet to take John's advice.

Tony Orlando & Dawn

The success of this pop trio originated with the song "Candida." First recorded by the Dawn duet, solo artist Tony Orlando voiced over the track in his own studio and released it. When that version climbed to number 3, the two forces agreed to unite. They went on to record several hits including "Knock Three Times" and "Tie a Yellow Ribbon Round the Ole Oak Tree," and had their own hit TV series on CBS.

Chicago

Chicago mixed rock with jazzy horns, Latin percussion, and walls of harmonies to create exuberant pop gems like "Does Anybody Really Know What Time It Is" and "Beginnings" from the band's debut album, *The Chicago Transit Authority*. Shortening their name for the follow-up record, Chicago's popularity exploded with the release of *Chicago II*, which yielded two Top 10 hits: "Make Me Smile" and the ballad "Colour My World." Another biggie was "Saturday in the Park," off of *Chicago V* (1972). In 1973, *Chicago VI* also topped the charts with "Feelin' Stronger Every Day" and "Just You 'n' Me." At last count, the group was up to album number XXXII. If only they'd been as creative with album names as they were with their songs!

DON MCLEAN

A gifted and sensitive songwriter, Don McLean is best remembered for "American Pie," even though the song wasn't typical of his repertoire. With folk roots and a gift for lyrics, McLean had other memorable compositions such as "And I Love You So" and "Vincent," written in honor of Vincent van Gogh. Reportedly, McLean was the inspiration for "Killing Me Softly with His Song," which earned three Grammys for singer Roberta Flack in 1973.

THE CHI-LITES

These Chicago-based soul vocalists used layered harmonies and creamy falsettos to top the pop charts in the early 1970s. They recorded eleven Top 20 R&B hits, including "Have You Seen Her" and "Oh Girl."

Rod Stewart

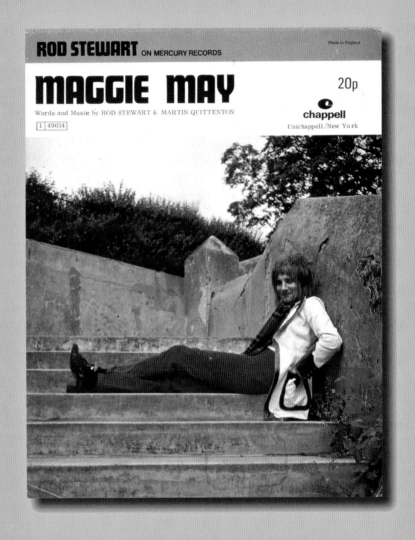

Blonde-headed London boy Rod Stewart always sounded like he had just blown his vocals out on the previous number, yet he never missed a note. After getting a professional start with the Jeff Beck Group, he joined up with bassist Ronnie Lane to form Small Faces (later known as Faces). Stewart's talents were in high form as a singer, songwriter, and charismatic frontman, and the band had a uniquely warm take on beat music and R&B—more raucous than the Beatles and more sensitive than the Stones. His successful solo career kicked off in 1969, reaching a creative high point three years later on *Every Picture Tells a Story*, which included the huge hit "Maggie May."

Carole King

Carole King's honest voice and eloquent piano playing—and her years working as a professional songwriter with partner/husband Gary Goffin—made her 1971 album *Tapestry* an enormous success. It stayed on the charts for six years (yes cousins, six *years*), won four Grammys including Best Album, and sold millions worldwide on the strength of classics like "You've Got a Friend" and "It's Too Late."

Lennon's international hit had also come on the heels of the Beatles' formal break-up in 1970 (see page 247). One of their last singles was "Let It Be," another soulful urging of peace. For fans, the song served a kind of dual purpose: it was a spiritual salve to our social problems that also seemed to carry a subtext about the Beatles calling it quits. The song worked on both levels, as if saying to listeners, "It's all over now. We still have questions, and we're not quite right just yet, but that's okay. There will be an answer. Let it be."

While we're on the topic, there was yet another potent, post-Beatles paean to peace: George Harrison's album *All Things Must Pass*. Beatles releases usually included just one or two songs each by George and Ringo (other Beatles originals were credited to Lennon/McCartney.)

The "quiet" Beatle had saved up some fantastic tunes. The album earned him a number 1 hit with "My Sweet Lord" in 1970 and was chock-full of other gorgeous, acoustic-driven songs like "Isn't It a Pity," "Beware of Darkness," "What Is Life," and "If Not For You."

As fate would have it, a court decided in 1976 that "My Sweet Lord" infringed on the copyright of "He's So Fine," the 1963 hit from the Chiffons. It wasn't hard to hear the similarity, though even the presiding judge acknowledged that musicians might borrow unintentionally from something they had heard at some point before.

No court ruling could take anything away from George, who was a deep well of original talent. I had played the Chiffons' song in the '60s and I played George's song in the '70s.

A Slice of American History

Artists of the early 1970s headed into a new decade with the 1960s in their rearview. It was a time to look back over all that had come before and then point yourself toward the future.

Don McLean wrote an epitaph to the bygone era in his epic song "American Pie." Much has been said and written about what exactly Don meant in that song (though when asked he joked, "It means I never have to work again," according to his biography). Because

he dedicated the *American Pie* album to Buddy Holly, it seemed a natural fit that "the father, son, and Holy Ghost" referred to Holly, Ritchie Valens, and J. P. "the Big Bopper" Richardson," who had died in a never-to-be-forgotten 1959 plane crash.

But McLean was a poet, and I have to figure that "the day the music died" was not a single day but a metaphor for the end of an epoch. The song collapses the entire social, political, and musical history of rock & roll's early days into an eight-and-a-half-minute song (we played a shortened version of it on AM radio). In it we hear echoes of lost leaders, of drug culture, of questioning religion, and even of America's tension with communism.

"American Pie" is the voice of one young man—an inward-looking individual at the dawn of the "me" decade—reflecting on an entire nation's recent past. The song is a bookend on the youth revolution and rock & roll's early days. They had been crushingly sad and joyously liberating all at once. And now, once again, it was time to move on.

The Eagles

Eric Clapton

Carly Simon

The Doobie Brothers

CHAPTER 8

1972–1973

Lions at the 'Gate

By now, all of my cousins know that I see rock & roll as a mirror. Who we are and what we go through, in good times and bad, is echoed in our music. It can be the center of your life—and it's certainly been at the heart of my own—but rock & roll doesn't live a life of its own. Music is a reflector, not a projector.

As the 1960s took on the soft glow of memory, mainstream music continued softening as well. Yet, in terms of style, the mainstream had also become very broad. The breakdown of social, racial, and gender barriers had intensified our curiosity about alternate perspectives, and on the pop charts you could discern the whole rainbow of American culture. For example, some decidedly *white* artists like the Osmonds, Ricky Nelson, and the Carpenters were on the charts right alongside the Jacksons, Al Green, and Aretha Franklin. Urban sounds by the likes of Chicago and the O'Jays were matched by rural, nature-lovin' tree-huggers like John Denver and Jackson Browne. We were also open to male and female artists alike, evidenced by the superstardom of Paul Simon and Marvin Gaye at the same time as Helen Reddy and Roberta Flack. There was something for everyone in those soft-hued hits of the early 1970s.

SEALS & CROFTS

This soft rock duo's "Summer Breeze" was a dreamy ode to warm weather. The multi-talented Jim Seals and Dash Crofts were considered one of the most successful acts in their genre, and broke the Top 10 with their albums *Summer Breeze* and *Diamond Girl*.

Diamonds in the Rough

How can it be that an era marked by mistrust and disgust produced so much lighthearted music? Richard Nixon is the face of the 1970s—not exactly the face you want staring back at you in an album full of memories, I know, but the Watergate scandal, the unpopular war in Vietnam, and Nixon's resignation defined the decade. That was our reality. And still we were singing about "Saturday in the Park" (Chicago) and "Puppy Love" (Donny Osmond).

I have a theory, and it's based on a little formula. I've always said that we'd have a beautiful world if people could hold on to just forty percent of their ideals and leave sixty percent of their energy for work and surviving everyday life. That may sound a little cold and capitalist, but I think most people past the age of thirty or so would agree. We should never let go of our basic ideals and dreams, but life exacts a toll from us. We don't live in utopia—the world is a tough place.

By the early '70s we'd grown older, with all of the luxuries and sacrifices that come with age, and our idealism was starting to be soft-pedaled with

DAVID BOWIE

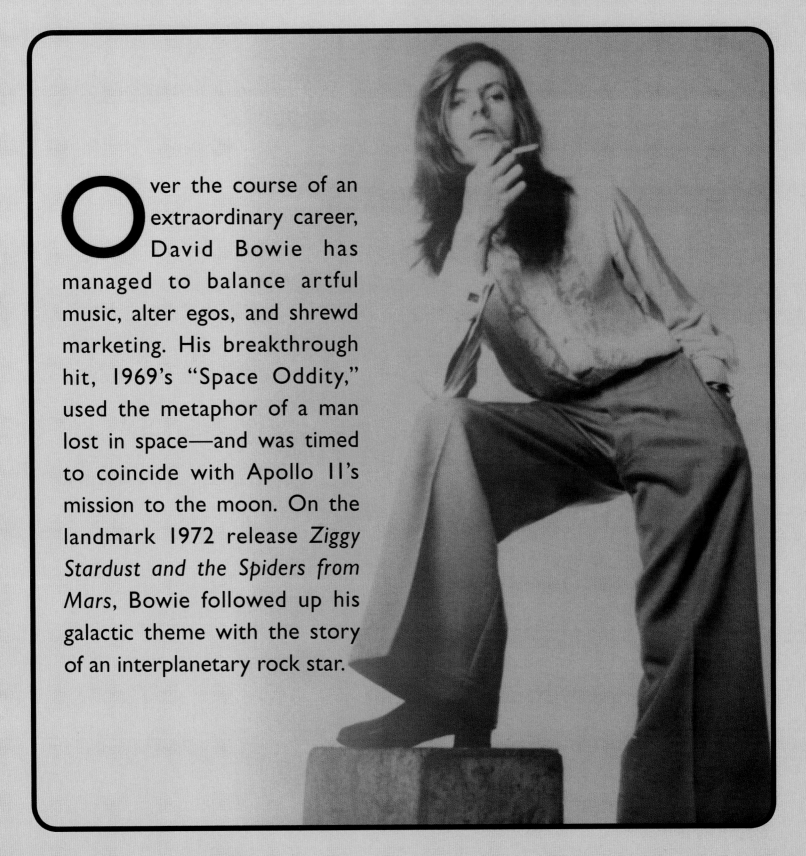

Over the course of an extraordinary career, David Bowie has managed to balance artful music, alter egos, and shrewd marketing. His breakthrough hit, 1969's "Space Oddity," used the metaphor of a man lost in space—and was timed to coincide with Apollo 11's mission to the moon. On the landmark 1972 release *Ziggy Stardust and the Spiders from Mars*, Bowie followed up his galactic theme with the story of an interplanetary rock star.

Arlo Guthrie

The eldest son of Woody Guthrie established his own folk legend with "Alice's Restaurant Massacree," which used satire to decry the misjudgment of 1960s American youth. In Arlo's 1967 song—as in Arlo's real-life experience—the narrator finds himself on trial for littering in front of a judge who is literally blind. The eighteen-minute song comes across the radio waves every year on Thanksgiving, that most American of holidays.

soft music. It was that 40/60 trade-off. We could still shake a leg to "Stuck in the Middle with You" (Stealers Wheel) or "Long Train Running" (the Doobie Brothers), but the hard-rockin' songs were outnumbered by the softies. It was the time of "Drift Away" (Dobie Gray), "Diamond Girl" (Seals & Crofts), and "Danny's Song" (Anne Murray, covering the original by Loggins and Messina). For Pete's sake, Michael Jackson was singing to a pet rat in "Ben"! It hadn't been long ago that James Brown sang "Get Up" and Eric Clapton sang "After Midnight"—now the big hit was the Fifth Dimensions' "Last Night I Didn't Get to Sleep at All."

So maybe were we just getting tired. Nobody was giving up, but it's fair to say we were slowing down a little bit. We were no longer the inexhaustable, invulnerable teenagers we had been. In our music we sought the same thing we sought in our lives: a safe haven. A comfort zone. For years we had been out there breathing the smoke and fire of revolution; now it was time to take in some fresh air and blue skies.

In the classic image of a soldier marching home from war, he's welcomed into the arms of his hometown girl (who will join him once again under that old apple tree, to borrow a song line). While we were out fighting intellectual and social revolutions, what did we leave waiting back home? Romance. Mainstream rock & roll had put romance on hold. We'd been too busy in those years of changing the world to sing about affection, but now we were washed over by a warm wave of songs about love lost and gained. Roberta Flack, a reigning queen of romance, wrapped us in her silky voice with hits including "Killing Me Softly," "Where Is the Love" (with Donny Hathaway), and the incomparable "The First Time Ever I Saw Your Face." Al Green, a king to Roberta's queen, had "Look What You Done for Me," "I'm Still In Love with You," and "Let's Stay Together." The list goes on forever, and we've stayed committed to these songs for years: "Oh Girl" (the Chi-Lites), "Sealed with a Kiss" (Bobby Vinton), "Everything I Own" (Bread), "Precious and Few" (Climax), and that quintessential '70s heartbreaker, "Alone Again (Naturally)" (Gilbert O'Sullivan).

The return of romance was like a turning back of the clocks. Before things

Cat Stevens

Unlike many British pop musicians, Londoner Cat Stevens drew more inspiration from classical music and old English folk songs than from American blues. The result was pristine folk-rock, as heard in the delicate "Moonshadow," "Morning Has Broken," and "Peace Train" from 1971's *Teaser and the Firecat.*

CARLY SIMON

With her sexy smile, and powerful voice, Carly Simon brought an easy glamour to the singer-songwriter era. Her debut album, *Carly Simon*, yielded the dramatic hit "That's the Way I've Always Heard It Should Be." In 1972 she cut "You're So Vain" with Mick Jagger singing backup, and it became an international smash. Simon has steadfastly refused to confirm the identity of the song's subject, although most of us know who it is.

got messy around 1963, popular music had been full of uncomplicated lyrics and easy melodies. We weren't about to go back to the starched-white collars and *Leave It to Beaver* mentality of the 1950s, but in the romantic tunes of the early 1970s we did embrace simple pleasures once again. It had been a long time coming.

Can't Stop the Rhythm

Soft rock shared the charts with soft R&B. But while most chart-topping rock artists were mellowing out, plenty of soul artists were getting gutsy. Sometimes their songs reflected the ongoing struggle of inner-city life, and sometimes they were just laying down great grooves to celebrate life. The Staples Singers had "I'll Take You There," War sang "Slippin' Into Darkness," and Bill Withers had the sultry "Use Me." Wonderful Stevie Wonder had "Superstition" and "Higher Ground." Billy Preston (whose keyboard work is heard all over the Beatles' last record, *Let It Be*) sung "Will It Go Round in Circles" and "Outa-Space," and Dr. John growled through "Right Place, Wrong Time."

Of course, romance remained the

Unfortunate Sons

I f America's involvement in the Vietnam War goes down in history as a terrible shame, a still greater disgrace is how our soldiers were treated when they returned home. These young men, many of them from the country's poorest neighborhoods, had put their lives on the line because our nation had asked them to. The ones lucky enough to make it home alive would never be the same again. And yet, instead of being thanked for their honorable, brave, and patriotic service, they were spit on and greeted with jeers. It was so terribly un-American that they never got the welcome home they deserved.

Whenever I make mention on the air at SIRIUS XM Radio of the reprehensible way our veterans were treated, I receive dozens of phone calls from 'Nam vets. They're always exceedingly gracious, and thank me for standing up for them. To me, these voices on the phone are a powerful reminder that American soldiers are to be treated with respect and honor.

stock and trade of R&B artists. You could hear the pillow talk (between a few tears on the pillow) in classics like Stevie's "You Are the Sunshine of My Life" and Marvin's "Let's Get It On." Then there were those aching love songs by Gladys Knight and the Pips, including "Neither One of Us (Wants to Be the First to Say Goodbye)" and "Midnight Train to Georgia."

One-Hit Wonderful

Across the spectrum, hit artists were mastering the two-and-a-half-minute format of AM radio. Each song on the Top 100 was like a perfect little treat for listeners to unwrap and savor for a moment before it quickly faded out, replaced in seconds by the next cut. I'm not so cynical as to characterize the trend as formulaic, but industry pros were certainly learning how to work the system. Record producers, managers, and the artists themselves came to recognize the power and potential of a single hit song.

In this musical environment, the rock & roll charts were starting to be peppered with a whole bunch of "one-hit wonders"—that is, major hits from

Todd Rundgren

Many will remember 1972's "Hello, It's Me" as an example of pure pop perfection, but there was always more to Todd Rundgren than met the ear. After leaving the British Invasion–inspired quartet the Nazz, this gifted Philadelphian launched a career exploring the full potential of his skills as a songwriter, guitarist, and producer.

Grand Funk Railroad

Discarded by critics but adored by fans, this "American Band" was one of the first to introduce hard rock in the late '60s, and became a commercial smash in the '70s. Much more rock than funk, their name derived from the Grand Trunk Railroad, a train line running through their hometown of Flint, Michigan.

artists you'd never heard of before and never would again. The one-hit wonder had long been a phenomenon in country music circles, where a single song could launch a singer to stardom and guarantee a lifelong gig at the Grand Ol' Opry (the Nashville temple of all that is holy in country music). Recognizing that scoring just one huge hit was like striking oil, people in the music biz started to drill. Spouting up from nowhere came a slew of one-hitters, including "Brandy" (Looking Glass), "Everybody Plays the Fool" (Main Ingredient), "Go All the Way" (Rasberries), "It Never Rains in Southern California" (Albert Hammond), and "Hocus Pocus" (by Focus—really!).

I've always thought it was strange that these artists could make such an impression with their songs though we seldom heard from them again. But that was the nature of an industry that was looking for quick sales of 45 rpm singles. The suit-and-tie businessmen behind those hits weren't always interested in nurturing a band's career or supporting a talented songwriter. With a minimal investment—not much more than a few thousand dollars for recording and distributing a single—they could rake in

Harry Chapin

A folk-rock artist from Brooklyn, New York, Harry Chapin climbed the charts with emotional singles like "Taxi" and "Cat's in the Cradle." Chapin also became known for his humanitarian and philanthropic efforts, co-founding the organization *World Hunger Year* with deejay Bill Ayres.

ALICE COOPER

Alice Cooper, seated, second from left

With a focus on theatrics and costumes during the age of peace and bell bottoms, Alice Cooper (born Vincent Damon Furnier, 1948) pioneered a brand of music later known as "shock rock." His biggest hits: "I'm Eighteen" and "School's Out."

The Allman Brothers

Formed in 1969 in Jacksonville, Florida, the Allman Brothers are the long-reigning kings of southern rock. With elements of blues, jazz, and R&B, the band quickly gained critical acclaim for their marathon concerts and exploring improvisations.

STEELY DAN

The two purveyors of perfection behind Steely Dan are guitarist Walter Becker and keyboardist-vocalist Donald Fagen. But as every Dan fan knows, they are famous for drawing on the world's finest session musicians to fill out their sophisticated songs and intricate arrangements. Despite the unique, revolving-door approach to band lineups, the Steely Dan sound is unmistakable on radio staples like "Reelin' in the Years," "My Old School," and "Rikki Don't Lose That Number."

millions. This takes nothing away from the music itself, of course (though it left more than a few one-hit artists in tatters). It shows the power of music to reach out and grab us emotionally. There was something in each of those songs that opened us up even when we had no connection to the artist, as we did with so many more enduring heroes of rock & roll. It's something like the experience of talking to a stranger on a bus: You have this anonymous relationship that provides an unusual brand of safety and comfort. When you're in that safe place, you can let your emotions flow. We all want to express ourselves.

Heavy Hitters

While an emphasis on poppy hit singles dominated the AM radio waves, hardrock artists were getting most of their airplay on the FM side. With the luxury of playing longer cuts and exploring tracks deep into an album, FM programmers were helping to foster longterm careers among their favorite artists. Bands like Faces, Pink Floyd, Joe Walsh, Deep Purple, Grand Funk Railroad, the Rolling Stones, Traffic, the J. Geils Band, Led Zeppelin, and Emerson, Lake & Palmer

The O'Jays

This Philadelphia soul quartet sang through the 1970s with enormous success. Smooth vocals and catchy lyrics helped the O'Jays solidify their place as a soul classic, landing big hits like "Back Stabbers," "Love Train," and "Use Ta Be My Girl."

Movies of the Early 1970s

Ryan O'Neal and Ali MacGraw get close in **Love Story.**

By this time in movie history, there were few restraints on what you could see onscreen. Directors were having a field day and we went right along with them.

In Don Siegel's *Dirty Harry,* Clint Eastwood showed how persuasive a .44 Magnum could be, while Stanley Kubrick's futuristic *A Clockwork Orange* orchestrated gang violence to Beethoven symphonies. William Friedkin's *The Exorcist,* starring Linda Blair, shocked audiences, and who can forget the backwoods nightmare that awaited Burt Reynolds and Jon Voight in John Boorman's *Deliverance.*

This was also the era of the special effects–laden "disaster" films, which usually placed a group of by-the-numbers characters in peril. The trick was to guess who was going to meet their doom next. It was all good fun as we watched Jacqueline Bissett and Dean Martin ride the unfriendly skies in *Airport,* Gene Hackman and Stella Stevens get that sinking feeling in *The*

Poseidon Adventure, Steve McQueen and Paul Newman teeter on the edge in *The Towering Inferno*, and more.

Meanwhile, Ali MacGraw and Ryan O'Neal captured each other's hearts, and ours, in *Love Story* while Liza Minnelli and director Bob Fosse ushered in a new style of movie musical with *Cabaret*. Paul Newman and Robert Redford teamed up again to pull off the ultimate con in *The Sting,* while Barbra Streisand romanced Robert Redford in *The Way We Were,* a ten tissue flick.

An up-and-coming director made us an offer we couldn't refuse, or resist. Francis Ford Coppola's *The Godfather*, with Marlon Brando as Don Vito Corleone, became an instant classic. It won Best Picture and made Al Pacino, as Michael Corleone, a star. It is considered one of the best movies of all time. Meanwhile, Robert de Niro, who played the young Vito Corleone in the equally brilliant sequel, *Godfather II,* had recently begun his long and successful collaboration with director Martin Scorsese in *Mean Streets.*

Hollywood was also experimenting with new genres. "Blaxploitation" films reached the mainstream with *Shaft* and *Superfly,* while martial arts superstar Bruce Lee showed off his mastery in *Enter the Dragon.*

When George C. Scott strapped on

James Caan, Marlon Brando, Al Pacino, and John Cazale mean business in **The Godfather.**

pearl-handle revolvers in *Patton,* a terrific film about the flamboyant General George S. Patton, he won the Best Actor Oscar and superstar status. The same happened to Gene Hackman, who also won an Oscar in the gritty detective drama *The French Connection.*

It was a very exciting time for moviemakers and audiences. I also am very happy to say that the awful, and I do mean awful, rock & roll films of the 1950s and early 1960s finally ran their course into oblivion. Because a little black box with a screen in our living rooms was showing us all kinds of programming for free, Hollywood smelled "Trouble in River City." The movie industry awoke to the realization that in order to survive, it finally had to deliver quality movies for all audience segments, and in the early 1970s, that's what we enjoyed.

ABOVE: *Passengers won't forget this New Year's Eve party in* **The Poseidon Adventure.** **LEFT:** *Gene Hackman stops a perp in* **The French Connection.**

Triumph and Tragedy in the World of Sports

Billie Jean King

The Battle of the Sexes was fought on a Houston tennis court in 1973 between self-anointed "male chauvinist" Bobby Riggs and women's tennis powerhouse Billie Jean King. Even at age fifty-five, claimed Riggs—who had been a top men's player in the 1940s—he could whip the best female player in the world. An estimated fifty million people tuned in to watch King beat Riggs decisively, scoring a victory for women's sports and a total knockout for feminism. Another exciting sports moment was Mark Spitz winning a then-record seven gold medals at the 1972 Munich Olympic Games. The joyful mood of the games was tragically ruined, however, when members of the Israeli Olympic team were taken hostage and killed by Black September, a militant Palestinian liberation group. This was the subject of the major motion picture, *Munich*.

The Doobie Brothers

The Doobie Brothers set the template for classic rock with mellow boogie grooves, bluesy guitar, and sweet country-influenced harmonies. The band's second album, *Toulouse Street*, brought them mainstream success with "Listen to the Music" and "Jesus Is Just Alright." The 1974 album *What Were Once Vices Are Now Habits* gave the band its number 1 single "Black Water."

weren't dependent on the quick-fix success of a single.

For players like these, a major hit could be the kiss of death, since devoted fans might accuse them of selling out. Mind you, they were making plenty of money; these guys were still cogs in the music industry's giant machine, though that fact was more easily hidden since they were adhering to a different business model. They might not have been "selling out" their art, but they were selling out concert halls, tee shirt stands, and record stores. Once again we see another example of "the man" making money on the long-haired kid. A pretty penny awaited those long-haired kids, too—call it backdoor capitalism.

Several AOR artists did manage to straddle the fence and appeal to listeners on the AM dial with an occasional piece of polished pop (Elton John, the Steve Miller Band, and Neil Young all come to mind), but they did so at great risk to their credibility. To this day, it seems some fans feel there is no greater crime an artist can commit than becoming a smashing success.

Feeling Fine Again

To my ears, the aggressive sound of

Nixon and the Watergate Burglary

When five men were arrested for breaking into Democratic party headquarters at the Watergate office complex in Washington, DC, no one could have anticipated that this small crime would topple the president—and permanently undo the public's faith in leadership. Investigation of the 1972 burglary uncovered that President Nixon's administration was involved in all kinds of skullduggery, from campaign fraud and political espionage to illegal wiretapping on a massive scale. A secret slush fund was used to pay the operatives who carried out "Tricky Dick's" dirty schticks. Mounting evidence forced Nixon to turn over recordings that directly implicated him in the cover-up of the Watergate break-in. Under threat of impeachment, Nixon on August 9, 1974, became the first and only president to resign. His vice president, Gerald Ford, became president—and, in his first major act as president, pardoned Nixon, which spared him from criminal prosecution. In case anyone out there wonders why we all grew so cynical about the government… that's the story!

THE ZOMBIES

THE ZOMBIES

While other groups were banging out bright little numbers on electric guitars, these world-class songwriters found their own sound on minor-key tunes driven by Rod Argent's organ and piano. They scored big on hits like "She's Not There" and "Tell Her No" in the mid 1960s and, after a dry period, returned in 1969 with "Time of the Season."

Jethro Tull

Characterized by the distinctive antics and flute playing of front man Ian Anderson, Jethro Tull was equal parts hard rock and folk, though the two styles were well separated on their recordings. On 1971's *Aqualung*, they showcased lyrics on religion in society and gained commercial success through the title track and the single "Locomotive Breath."

ERIC CLAPTON
SLOWHAND

Eric Clapton

Blind Faith: *Clapton, at far right, is having a laugh as he and drummer Ginger Baker switch instruments.*

Eric Clapton, the most popular guitarist of all time, is revered by six-stringers for having introduced the guitar work of African American blues musicians to white audiences. In doing so, he was fundamentally responsible for altering the direction of rock guitar. "EC" was the spotlight stealer in his many bands, including the Yardbirds, the Bluesbreakers, Cream, Blind Faith, and Derek & the Dominos (he was Derek), and he played countless sessions as a sideman—perhaps his most famous being an uncredited guitar solo on the Beatles' "While My Guitar Gently Weeps," written by friend George Harrison. Clapton kicked off his solo career in 1970 with a self-titled record that yielded a hit with the J.J. Cale song "After Midnight."

hard rock represented feelings left over from the '60s. These scrappy young guys weren't giving up the fight, and they appealed to those still youthful or angry enough to carry on the cause. They picked up the torch of revolution before it dropped to the ground, and they lit the way for a whole new generation.

But in the mainstream, we were cooling down. We were beating our swords into plow shafts, as the saying goes, and peacefully planting seeds for the future. Even at a time when we were living under a government that seemed to rule in a moral vacuum, you could hear a fresh, hopeful spirit.

When Johnny Nash sang "I Can See Clearly Now," it was like a rain had washed away all the sins of our nation's past. The group Argent (led by Rod Argent, formerly of the Zombies) told us it was time to "Hold Your Head Up," and the O'Jays implored listeners to get aboard the "Love Train." Newfound spirituality was woven into hit songs like "Mother and Child Reunion" by Paul Simon, "Give Me Love (Give Me Peace on Earth)" by George Harrison, "Day By Day" from the "rock opera" *Godspell*, and "I'd Like to Teach the World to Sing (In

America

Despite the name of this soft-rock/folk-rock group America was composed of three sons of American servicemen living in London. Their catchy lyrics and acoustic harmonies first hit the radiowaves in 1972 when "A Horse with No Name" rode them to the top of UK and US charts.

The Origins of Punk Rock

The prototype for punk was laid down by three crucial American bands: the Stooges, the Motor City Five (better known as MC5), and the Velvet Underground. In their eyes, rock & roll was supposed to be anti-establishment but had actually *become* the establishment. While the Velvet Underground was more avant-garde, the Stooges (led by Iggy Pop—shown right) and MC5 went for a raucous, extreme,

spittin'-mad version of deconstructed rock that made Elvis Presley look as conservative as Perry Como. Once the style made it across the Atlantic British bands like the Sex Pistols continued stripping away the warmth and R&B-based rhythm of rock & roll. Oddly enough punk was hugely influential on later artists who showed a great affinity for melody and pop sense, like the Clash the Ramones, Elvis Costello and the Pretenders

Perfect Harmony)"—a song that began as a jingle for Coca-Cola, but carried a message that resonated so strongly it became a hit for two different artists at the same time (the Hillside Singers, who are heard on the Coke commercial and the New Seekers).

A Closing Melody

Remember the good stuff and point your eyes toward the future—that's what we like to do. Our minds, maybe even our souls, have this kind of mechanism built in to protect us from the memories that hurt a little too much. We don't erase them entirely, but we file them away. It's a good ol' analog process, not a digital deletion. When I reflect on days gone by, I don't think first of Joe McCarthy or Kent State or Richard Nixon. I'll never forget what we've been through, and our nation has to live with those scars, but my mind wanders instead to sunshine at the beach and innocent fun with friends. School days and easier times.

The opening lines of Bill Withers' "Lean on Me," a tribute to friendship and brotherhood, did a beautiful job

PINK FLOYD

In the late '60s and early '70s, Pink Floyd became known for exploring the outermost fringes of psychedelic rock. But anyone who figured they were too far beyond the mainstream to connect with big audiences was in for a big surprise. In 1973, Floyd released the landmark *Dark Side of the Moon*, which was a mainstay on Billboard charts for—are you ready for this?—*1,500 weeks.* That's more than twenty-eight years.

The Eagles

Remember the good stuff and point your eyes toward the future.

Formed in 1970, the Eagles chose their band name in honor of the Byrds. Like the Byrds, they melded country influences and delicate harmonies in rock music that expressed both the sunny side and the dark underbelly of the California dream. The 1976 album *Their Greatest Hits (1971–1975)*—which includes everything from "Take It Easy" and "Witchy Woman" to "Lyin' Eyes" and the precious "The Best of My Love"—is still the best-selling album ever in the US, with about 29 million copies sold as of early 2009.

of summing up where we were at this moment in time. Before signing off, I'd like to leave you with Bill Withers' timeless lyrics:

Sometimes in our lives
We all have pain
We all have sorrow
But if we are wise
We know that there's
Always tomorrow

I hope you'll always have a friend to lean on. Even when there's no one else around, you can forever find comfort in music. Peace to you, cousins.

COUSIN BRUCIE SIGNS OFF

As I sit here putting the last of my rock & roll memories down on paper for this book, I'm awestruck by how much we've all been through. Frankly, it amazes me that we ever survived. It's pretty incredible that the train we were riding on never went completely off the rails. Our leaders were, by and large, asleep at the wheel through some very difficult days, and we kept chugging forward only on the steam of the "everyman." That's you and me, cousins, even more so than our bygone heroes and rock & roll stars.

We persevered and made the world a better place in the face of profound fear of change. What was that all about, anyway? Wasn't our country founded on the right to change, the desire to change, and a fearless navigation of the new?

While I can certainly understand rolling your eyes at the antics of a younger generation, or plugging your ears to their music, I don't see why we are always so slow to embrace change. Even faced with something clearly better than what we've had before—whether it's a new sound, a new remote control, or a new president—we tend to prefer familiarity.

We may never get a satisfactory answer to why we went down some of the dark paths we did, like why we were in Vietnam, why John F. Kennedy was killed, or why it took such a painfully long time to get a dialog going between America's races, cultures, and creeds. However, I'm very optimistic about where the world is headed. Always have been. I have great confidence in the power of the human spirit and in our nation. I believe that the best way always finds a way.

I hope the past few hundred pages have served as a reminder of where we've been, because only by reflecting on all of the obstacles we've overcome

Young people are the dreamers, and unless we go terribly wrong, there will be new generations to imagine an ever-brighter future.

can we appreciate where we are in the present. Awareness of the past is not just for the generation that lived through it, either: The lessons of our lives are what we have to pass along to our children. I think that's the wisdom in "standing on the shoulders of giants." We are the giants! Ask your kids to hop on your back, look out over the future, and tell you what's coming next. They will change the conversation in the nation as we once did.

We can age gracefully and still take a lesson from the young poets, the new soldiers of change. Listen to the poets. Young people are the dreamers, and unless we go terribly wrong there will be new generations to imagine an ever-brighter future.

And the beat goes on....

Cousins! My publisher Charlie Nurnberg called me and asked, "Brucie, where is Billy Joel, Bruce Springsteen, Fleetwood Mac, the Cars, Cheap Trick, and ABBA? Why aren't they in the book? I thought for a while and answered him, "Charlie, you just gave me my next book!" And Those Hits Just Keep On Coming!

ROCK & ROLL DICTIONARY

A gas: a lot of fun

All show no go: a fancy car that doesn't actually drive very fast, or a girl

Ankle biters: small children

Ape: (eg, to "go ape") to go irate or crazy, as in "My dad will go ape when he sees my grades."

BA: bare ass

Bad: awesome

Badass: a tough guy or reckless character, someone you don't want to mess with

Bag: what you did or liked was "your bag"

Ball: to party or have a good time, later evolved into a term for sex

Birth control seats: bucket seats in a car

Bitchin': something good or exciting

Blast: a great time

Blow the doors off: to have a rocking time

Blitzed: drunk

Bogart: to hog something

Bone yard: junkyard

Boogie: to leave a scene discreetly, as in "This place is a drag, I'm going to boogie."

Boss: great or cool, as in "This new album is boss."

Bread: money

Brew: beer

Bug out: to leave the area

Bummed out: depressed

Bummer: a disappointment

Burn rubber: to accelerate quickly so that the tires spin in place, burning the rubber

Cat: a guy

Cherry: pristine, perfectly neat, virgin

Chick: a girl

Choice: very cool or good, as in "His new car is really choice."

Chop: to degrade verbally

Chrome dome: a bald guy

Church key: the tool used to open beer or soda cans before the invention of "pop tops"

Cool: nice or "neat"

Cool head: nice guy

Cooties: an invisible infection that someone who wasn't cool had

Copacetic: very good, all right

Crash: go to bed or go to sleep

Cruising: driving up and down the street with no real purpose, often looking for girls or races

Daddy's car: a car typical of an older or more conservative person

Decked out: dressed up for an occasion, as in "We were really decked out for prom."

Dibs: used to claim rights to something, as in "I've got dibs on that last slice of pizza."

Dig: to understand

Ditz: someone who isn't smart

Don't flip your wig: used to tell someone to relax

Don't have a cow: used to tell someone to relax

Don't sweat it: don't worry about it

Downer: someone or something who brings the mood down

Drag: something that is boring

Fab: great or fantastic

Far out: awesome

Fink: a tattletale, a rat

Five-finger discount: stealing; "He didn't pay for the candy bar, he took the five finger discount."

Five-oh-two: a term for drunk driving; 502 was the penal code

Flake: someone unreliable

Flat-top: a short haircut often cut very close and even at the top

Flat-top with fenders: a flat-top with long sides

Flee the scene: to leave somewhere in a hurry

Flower child: hippie

Fox: a very attractive girl or woman

Freak out: temporary loss of control; an attack of nerves or anxiety

Funky: a term for cool that also can mean rotten as in "this milk is funky, how old is it?"

Fuzz: the police, as in "Let's cut out, I think the fuzz are coming."

Get it together: compose yourself

Gimme some skin: give me a high-five; shake hands with me

Going steady: dating one person exclusively

Greaser: someone who used a lot of grease in his hair

Gremmy: a novice surfer

Groovy: nice or cool

Groady: dirty, ugly, or undesirable; an abbreviation of grotesque

Hawk: someone with pro-war beliefs

Hang loose: to relax

Haul ass: to drive extremely fast or "Let's get out of here."

Heartthrob: a teen idol

Heat: the police

Heavy: deep or profound; "That new album is heavy."

Hip: very good, cool

Hodad: someone who hangs around the beach but doesn't surf

Hook: to rob or steal

Hunk: an attractive, typically strong man

Ivy Leaguers: men's pants made of polished cotton, no pleats, and with a buckle in the back

Jazzed: excited

Jump bad: to look for a fight, as in "That guy is bad news; he tries to jump bad with everyone."

Kibosh: to put a stop to, to end something

Kiss up: someone who strives to please a teacher or authority figure; a teacher's pet

Lay it on me: just say it, encouraging someone to deliver the news

Mover: someone with a plan, someone driven

Nifty: neat or cool, generally used by someone who wasn't very cool

On the make: someone looking hard for a girlfriend or boyfriend

Out of sight: fantastic, awesome

Peach: someone very nice or sweet

Pad: a house or apartment

Pin: to stare, or to nail someone in a negative way

Pits: something bad or awful, as in "This movie is the pits."

Rag top: a convertible with a roll-down cloth top (as opposed to a removable hard top)

Right on: a way of saying "I agree."

Righteous: extremely good or fine; beautiful

Rip off: to cheat someone out of money or get them to pay too much for something

Scheming: really interested in a member of the opposite sex; "He is really scheming on her."

Score: to obtain; "Let's score some beer."; or to make a sexual conquest

Screwed up: made a mistake; something unorganized; chaotic

Shades: sunglasses

Skirt: girl

Skuzz: ugly, undesirable

Solid: reliable, all right

Spiffy: neat

Square: someone not cool, typically a geek or adult

Threads: clothing

Tough toenails: a way of saying "Too bad."

What's your bag, man? to ask "What's happening?" or "What do you do?"

Woody wagon: a station wagon with wood sidings used to transport surfboards

Zap: wipe out or defeat

COUSIN BRUCIE'S 250 MOST INFLUENTIAL ARTISTS

Music is not a competitive sport, and I've always believed there's room for everyone. But every now and then I'm asked for my "top" this or "most favorite" that. For the cousins out there who need to know, here are 250 of the artists and songs I believe to be among the most influential in the golden age of rock & roll music, from the time the clock started to rock in 1954 through to 1973. I know it's not a complete list, but I think you'll agree that these were all big players. I've also included just one song from each artist (listed alphabetically) to get you humming along, plus the year that hit made its run up the charts. As always, feel free to add your own favorites. **Cousins, remember this list is alphabetical!**

1. Aerosmith "Dream On," 1973
2. The Allman Brothers Band "Ramblin' Man," 1973
3. America "Horse with No Name," 1972
4. The Animals "The House of the Rising Sun," 1964
5. Paul Anka "Diana," 1957
6. Argent "Hold Your Head Up," 1972
7. The Association "Along Comes Mary," 1966
8. Frankie Avalon "Venus," 1958
9. Badfinger "Come and Get It," 1970
10. Joan Baez "The Night They Drove Old Dixie Down," 1971
11. The Band "Up on Cripple Creek," 1969
12. The Beach Boys "Surfin' USA," 1963
13. The Beatles "I Want to Hold Your Hand," 1964
14. The Beau Brummels "Just a Little," 1965
15. Jeff Beck "Beck's Bolero," 1968
16. The Bee Gees "Massachusetts," 1967
17. Harry Belafonte "Jamaica Farewell," 1957
18. Chuck Berry "Maybellene," 1955
19. Black Sabbath "War Pigs," 1969
20. Blood, Sweat & Tears "You Make Me So Very Happy," 1969
21. Blue Cheer "Summertime Blues," 1968
22. David Bowie "Space Oddity," 1969
23. The Box Tops "The Letter," 1967
24. Bread "Make It With You," 1970
25. James Brown "I Got You (I Feel Good)," 1965
26. Jackson Browne "Doctor, My Eyes," 1972
27. The Buckinghams "Kind of a Drag," 1967
28. The Byrds "Mr. Tambourine Man," 1965
29. Glen Campbell "By the Time I Get to Phoenix," 1967
30. Canned Heat "Goin' Up the Country," 1970
31. The Carpenters "We've Only Just Begun," 1970
32. Johnny Cash "Ring of Fire," 1956
33. The Chairmen of the Board "Give Me Just a Little More Time," 1970
34. The Chambers Brothers "Time Has Come Today," 1968

35. Harry Chapin "Taxi," 1972

36. Ray Charles "What'd I Say," 1959

37. Chubby Checker "The Twist," 1960

38. Chicago "Does Anybody Really Know What Time It Is?" 1970

39. The Chiffons "He's So Fine," 1963

40. The Chi-Lites "Oh, Girl," 1971

41. Lou Christie "The Gypsy Cried," 1963

42. Eric Clapton "After Midnight," 1970

43. Petula Clark "Downtown," 1965

44. The Classics IV "Stormy," 1968

45. The Coasters "Charlie Brown," 1958

46. Eddie Cochrane "Summertime Blues," 1958

47. Judy Collins "Both Sides Now," 1968

48. The Contours "Do You Love Me," 1962

49. Sam Cooke "You Send Me," 1957

50. Alice Cooper "School's Out," 1972

51. Country Joe and the Fish "Feel-Like-I'm-Fixin'-to-Die Rag," 1969

52. The Cowsills "The Rain, the Park and Other Things," 1967

53. Cream "Sunshine of Your Love," 1968

54. Creedence Clearwater Revival "Bad Moon Rising," 1969

55. Jim Croce "Time in a Bottle," 1972

56. Crosby, Stills, Nash & Young "Ohio," 1970

57. The Crystals "Then He Kissed Me," 1962

58. Bobby Darin "Splish Splash," 1958

59. The Dave Clark Five "Glad All Over," 1964

60. The Spencer Davis Group "Gimme Some Lovin'," 1966

61. Deep Purple "Hush," 1968

62. Delaney & Bonnie "Never Ending Song of Love," 1971

63. The Dells "Oh, What A Night," 1956

64. John Denver "Take Me Home, Country Roads," 1971

65. Neil Diamond "Kentucky Woman," 1966

66. Bo Diddley "Bo Diddley," 1999

67. Dion "Runaround Sue," 1960

68. Dr. Hook & the Medicine Show "The Cover of the Rolling Stone," 1973

69. Fats Domino "Blueberry Hill," 1956

70. Donovan "Sunshine Superman," 1966

71. The Doobie Brothers "Listen to the Music," 1972

72. The Doors "Light My Fire," 1966

73. The Drifters "There Goes My Baby," 1959

74. Bob Dylan "Like a Rolling Stone," 1965

75. The Eagles "Take It Easy," 1972

76. Duane Eddy "Rebel-Rouse," 1958

77. The Edgar Winter Group "Frankenstein," 1973

78. Dave Edmunds "I Hear You Knocking," 1970

79. Jonathan Edwards "Sunshine," 1971

80. The Electric Prunes "Too Much to Dream Last Night," 1967

81. The Everly Brothers "Bye Bye Love," 1957

82. José Feliciano "Light My Fire," 1968

83. The Fifth Dimension "Let the Sunshine In," 1969

84. Roberta Flack "The First Time Ever I Saw Your Face," 1972

85. The Fortunes "You've Got Your Troubles," 1965

86. The Four Seasons "Big Girls Don't Cry," 1962

87. The Four Tops "Baby I Need Your Lovin'," 1965

88. Connie Francis "Who's Sorry Now," 1958

89. Aretha Franklin "Respect," 1967

90. Free "All Right Now," 1970

91. Marvin Gaye "Ain't That Peculiar," 1963

92. Gerry & the Pacemakers "Don't Let The Sun Catch You Cryin'," 1964

93. Lesley Gore "It's My Party," 1963

94. Grand Funk Railroad "We're an American Band," 1973

95. The J. Geils Band "Looking for a Love," 1972

96. The Grassroots "Let's Live for Today," 1967

97. The Grateful Dead "Casey Jones," 1970

98. Dobie Gray "Drift Away," 1973

99. Al Green "Let's Stay Together," 1972

100. The Guess Who "These Eyes," 1969

101. Arlo Guthrie "The City of New Orleans," 1972

102. Bill Haley & His Comets "Rock Around the Clock," 1954

103. The Happenings "See You in September," 1966

104. George Harrison "What Is Life," 1970

105. Richie Havens "Here Comes the Sun," 1971

106. Isaac Hayes "Theme from *Shaft*," 1971

107. Jimi Hendrix "All Along the Watchtower," 1968

108. Herman's Hermits "Mrs. Brown You've Got a Lovely Daughter," 1965

109. The Hollies "Bus Stop," 1966

110. Buddy Holly and the Crickets "Peggy Sue," 1957

111. The Isley Brothers "It's Your Thing," 1962

112. The Jackson 5 "I Want You Back," 1970

113. Tommy James and the Shondells "I Think We're Alone Now," 1966

114. Jan & Dean "Dead Man's Curve," 1964

115. Jay and the Americans "Come A Little Bit Closer," 1964

116. Jefferson Airplane "Somebody To Love," 1967

117. Jethro Tull "Aqualung," 1971

118. Janis Joplin "Me & Bobby McGee," 1967

119. Elton John "Your Song," 1970

120. Tom Jones "What's New Pussycat," 1965

121. B.B. King "The Thrill Is Gone," 1970

122. Carole King "It's Too Late," 1971

123. The Kingston Trio "Tom Dooley," 1958

124. The Kingsmen "Louie, Louie" 1963

125. The Kinks "All Day and All of the Night," 1965

126. Gladys Knight & the Pips "Heard It Through the Grapevine," 1967

127. Kool and the Gang "Funny Stuff," 1973

128. Led Zeppelin "Whole Lotta Love," 1970

129. Brenda Lee "Sweet Nothing," 1960

130. John Lennon "Imagine," 1971

131. Gary Lewis and the Playboys "The Diamond Ring," 1965

132. Jerry Lee Lewis "Whole Lot of Shakin' Going On," 1957

133. Little Anthony & the Imperials "Tears on My Pillow," 1958

134. Little Richard "Tutti Frutti," 1956

135. Loggins & Messina "Your Momma Don't Dance," 1972

136. The Lovin' Spoonful "Do You Believe In Magic," 1965

137. Lulu "To Sir With Love," 1967

138. Frankie Lymon & the Teenagers "Why Do Fools Fall in Love," 1956

139. The Mamas and the Papas "California Dreamin'," 1966

140. Manfred Mann "Doo Wah Diddy Diddy," 1964

141. The Marvelletes "Please Mr. Postman," 1961

142. John Mayall's Blues Breakers with Eric Clapton "Hideaway"

143. Curtis Mayfield "Freddie's Dead" (Theme from *Superfly*), 1972

144. MC5 (Motor City Five) "Kick Out the Jams," 1969

145. Paul McCartney and Wings "My Love," 1973

146. The McCoys "Hang on Sloopy," 1965

147. Scott McKenzy "San Francisco (Be Sure to Wear Flowers in Your Hair)," 1967

148. Don McLean "American Pie," 1971

149. Clyde McPhatter "Treasure of Love," 1956

150. Melanie "Brand New Key," 1971

151. Harold Melvin and the Blue Notes "If You Don't Know Me By Now," 1972

152. The Steve Miller Band "The Joker," 1973

153. The Miracles featuring Bill "Smokey" Robinson "Shop Around," 1960

154. Moby Grape "Sittin' by the Window," 1967

155. The Monkees "Last Train to Clarksville," 1966

156. The Moody Blues "Knights in White Satin," 1967

157. Mott the Hoople "All The Young Dudes," 1972

158. Ricky Nelson "A Teenager's Romance," 1957

159. Wayne Newton "Daddy Don't You Walk So Fast," 1972

160. Nilsson "Everybody's Talkin'," 1969

161. The Nitty Gritty Dirt Band "Mr. Bojangles," 1971

162. The Ohio Express "Yummy Yummy Yummy," 1968

163. The O'Jays "Love Train," 1972

164. Roy Orbison "Crying," 1961

165. Tony Orlando & Dawn "Candida," 1970

166. The Osmonds "One Bad Apple," 1971

167. Gilbert O'Sullivan "Alone Again (Naturally)," 1972

168. The Partridge Family "I Think I Love You," 1970

169. Paul Revere & the Raiders "Kicks," 1966

170. Carl Perkins "Blue Suede Shoes," 1956

171. Peter and Gordon "A World Without Love," 1964

172. Peter, Paul & Mary "Puff the Magic Dragon," 1963

173. Wilson Pickett "Mustang Sally," 1965

174. Pink Floyd "Money," 1973

175. Gene Pitney "Town Without Pity," 1962

176. The Platters "With This Ring," 1966

177. Elvis Presley "Heartbreak Hotel," 1956

178. Billy Preston "Outa-Space," 1972

179. Procul Harum "A Whiter Shade of Pale," 1967

180. Gary Puckett & the Union Gap "Over You," 1968

181. The Rasberries "Go all The Way," 1972

182. The Rascals "Good Lovin'," 1966

183. Otis Redding "(Sittin' On) The Dock of the Bay," 1961

184. Martha Reeves & the Vandellas "Dancin' in the Street," 1964

185. The Righteous Brothers "Unchained Melody," 1965

186. Johnny Rivers "Memphis," 1964

187. Kenny Rogers & the First Edition "Ruby, Don't Take Your Love to Town," 1969

188. The Rolling Stones "(I Can't Get No) Satisfaction," 1966

189. The Ronettes "Be My Baby," 1963

190. Todd Rundgren "Hello, It's Me," 1973

191. Mitch Ryder & the Detroit Wheels "Jenny Takes A Ride," 1966

192. Sgt. Barry Sadler "The Ballad of the Green Berets," 1966

193. Sam and Dave "Soul Man," 1967

194. Santana "Evil Ways," 1970

195. Seals & Crofts "Summer Breeze," 1972

196. The Searchers "Don't Throw Your Love Away," 1964

197. Neil Sedaka "Breaking Up Is Hard to Do," 1962

198. The Seekers "Georgy Girl," 1966

199. The Serendipity Singers "Don't Let The Rain Come Down," 1964

200. The Shangri-La's "Leader of the Pack," 1964

201. Del Shannon "Little Town Flirt," 1963

202. The Shirelles "Dedicated to the One I Love," 1961

203. Simon & Garfunkel "The Sounds of Silence," 1966

204. Carly Simon "You're So Vain," 1973

205. Percy Sledge "When a Man Loves a Woman," 1966

206. Sly & the Family Stone "Dance to the Music," 1968

207. The Small Faces "Itchycoo Park," 1968

208. Sonny & Cher "I Got You, Babe," 1965

209. The Spinners "I'll Be Around," 1972

210. Spiral Starecase "More Today Than Yesterday," 1969

211. Dusty Springfield "I Only Want to Be With You," 1964

212. The Standells "Dirty Water," 1966

213. The Staple Singers "I'll Take You There," 1972

214. Steely Dan "Do It Again," 1973

215. Steppenwolf "Born to be Wild," 1968

216. Cat Stevens "Peace Train," 1971

217. Rod Stewart "Maggie May," 1971

218. The Stooges "I Wanna Be Your Dog," 1969

219. The Strawberry Alarm Clock "Incense and Peppermints," 1967

220. The Supremes "Where Did Our Love Go," 1964

221. The Sweet "Little Willy," 1973

222. T. Rex "Bang a Gong (Get It On)," 1972

223. Booker T. and the M.G.'s "Green Onions," 1962

224. James Taylor "Fire and Rain," 1970

225. The Temptations "My Girl," 1964

226. B.J. Thomas "Raindrops Keep Fallin' on My Head," 1968

227. Three Dog Night "One," 1969

228. Tower of Power "So Very Hard To Go," 1972

229. The Troggs "Wild Thing," 1966

230. The Turtles "Happy Together," 1965

231. Uriah Heep "Easy Livin'," 1972

232. Van Morrison "Brown-Eyed Girl," 1967

233. Vanilla Fudge "You Keep Me Hangin' On," 1968

234. Bobby Vee and the Strangers "Come Back When You Grow Up," 1967

235. The Velvet Underground "Femme Fatale," 1966

236. The Ventures "Hawaii Five-O," 1969

237. Gene Vincent "Be-Bop-a-Lula," 1956

238. Bobby Vinton "Roses Are Red (My Love)," 1962

239. Junior Walker and the All Stars "Shotgun," 1965

240. War (with Eric Burdon) "Spill the Wine," 1970

241. Dionne Warwick "Anyone Who Had a Heart," 1963

242. Mary Wells "You Beat Me to the Punch," 1962

243. The Who "Pinball Wizard," 1969

244. Jackie Wilson "Lonely Tear Drops," 1959

245. Stevie Wonder "Uptight (Everything's Alright)," 1966

246. The Yardbirds "Heart Full of Soul," 1965

247. Yes "Roundabout," 1971

248. Neil Young "Heart of Gold," 1972

249. Frank Zappa "Peaches en Regalia," 1969

250. The Zombies "Tell Her No," 1964

EPILOGUE

by Billy Joel

Oh man—Cousin Bruuuuucie!!!!! And all that fine harmony pouring out of all those tiny little transistor radios on a hot Sunday afternoon at Jones Beach—Parking Field #4, specifically, if you were "In with the In Crowd." And before the day was done, there we were in that long, dark echo chamber of a tunnel working out the vocals to "Speedo," "Come Go with Me," "In the Still of the Night," "Blue Moon," "Gloria,"

"Silhouettes," "So Much in Love," "Barbara Ann," "Denise," and "The Book of Love," just to name a few. We spent way more time studying falsetto and bass parts than we ever spent on algebra or chemistry. And why not? Singing those songs made our lives instantly sweeter and turned us into rock & roll stars—just for that moment. But oh, what a moment! We owned the tunnel and the boys' room and the locker room and the corner under the streetlamp. It wasn't much, I suppose, but it was ours. And back in the day, those small pieces of the world were kingdoms for us. And we were the kings.

Music was the language of the land, and Cousin Brucie was the man with the mike—giving us the good news day after day for a teenage eternity. And it seemed to last forever.

I tried to resurrect a little moment of that magic with an acappella recording of a song I wrote in 1983 called "For the Longest Time." And whaddaya know—it became a top 10 hit! In 1984!

And the same thing happened with a "slow dance" song I wrote based on an old piece by Ludwig Van that I called "This Night." And Kaboom! Top 40 in 1984! Crazy, man. How the hell does something like that happen? Cousin Brucie can tell you. Just listen—and groove.

—*Billy Joel*

BIBLIOGRAPHY

Alan, Howard. *The Don McLean Story: Killing Us Softly with His Songs*. London: Lulu Enterprises, 2007.

America's Story From America's Library, www.americaslibrary.gov

Audio Engineering Society (AES) publications, www.aes.org/publications/

Babiuk, Andy. *Beatles Gear*. San Francisco: Backbeat Books, 2001.

Billboard Historical Charts, www.billboard.com/bbcom/charts/yearend_chart_index.jsp

Bogdanov, Vladimir et al. *All Music Guide: The Definitive Guide to Popular Music*. Ann Arbor: AEC One Stop Group, 2001.

Brian Wilson website, www.brianwilson.com

Bright Tunes Music v. Harrisongs Music, 420 F. Supp. 177 (S.D.N.Y. 1976). Retrieved December 2008 at http://cip.law.ucla.edu/cases/case_brightharrisongs.html

The Chronicle of Higher Education, http://chronicle.com

Chronicle of the Cinema, edited by Robyn Karney. Dorling Kindersley, 1995

CNN archives, www.cnn.com/

Crypto Machines, http://jproc.ca/crypto/menu.html

First Sounds, http://firstsounds.org

Garofalo, Reebee. *Rockin' Out: Popular Music in the U.S.A.* Upper Saddle River, NJ: Pearson Prentice Hall, 2005.

Gordon, Lois and Alan Gordon. *American Chronicle: Year by Year Through the Twentieth Century*. New Haven: Yale University Press, 1999.

Haldeman, H. R. with Joseph DiMona. *The Ends of Power*. New York: Times Books, 1978.

History.com, www.history.com

Internet Movie Database, www.imdb.com

Kent State University archives, http://dept.kent.edu/sociology/lewis/lewihen.htm

King, Jr, Martin Luther. *The Measure of a Man (Facets)*. Minneapolis: Augsburg Fortress Publishers, 2001.

Larkin, Colin. *The Virgin Encyclopedia of Popular Music*. London: Virgin Books, 1997.

Library of Congress, www.loc.gov/index.html

Maloof, Rich. *Jim Marshall: The Father of Loud*. San Francisco: Backbeat Books, 2004.

Merseybeat ABD, www.merseybeatabd.co.uk/

Music Outfitters, www.musicoutfitters.com

The National Center for Public Policy Research, www.nationalcenter.org/

National Park Service, www.nps.gov/edis

National Public Radio archives, www.npr.org

Newquist, HP and Pete Prown. *Legends of Rock Guitar*. Milwaukee: Hal Leonard, 1997.

The New York Times archives, http://nytimes.com/

Shadwik, Keith. *Jimi Hendrix: Musician*. London: Backbeat Books, 2003.

Spector, Ronnie. *Be My Baby: How I Survived Mascara, Miniskirts, and Madness, or My Life as a Fabulous Ronette*. Chicago: Onyx Publishing Group, 2004

The Thomas Edison Papers, http://edison.rutgers.edu/

Time Magazine archives, www.time.com

United States Early Radio History, http://earlyradiohistory.us

Warner, Jay. *American Singing Groups*. New York: Da Capo Press, 1992.

WCBS Newsradio 880 archives, www.wcbs880.com

Whitburn, Joel. *Billboard Top 10 Album Carts, 1963–1998*. Menomenee Falls: Record Research, 1999.

White, Thomas H. *Jukebox Collections*, www.jukebox-collections.com

ACKNOWLEDGMENTS

Cousin Brucie Thanks...

To my parents, who will probably read this book if there is a lending library in Heaven—thanks Mom & Dad for always encouraging and believing in me.

To my brother Bob who, regardless of the weather, helped produce the legendary Palisades Park Shows for a decade—he was always there.

To my publishers Charlie Nurnberg and Jeremy Nurnberg for your enthusiasm and trust in me—this proves once again that great publishers produce great books.

Rich Maloof, my partner, you did it again—made my dreams and memories a wonderful reality. Thank you for your skill, sense of humor, and especially your appetite.

To the world's best lawyer, Judy Tint. Thanks for the vigil, and always being there for me. To f-Stop Fitzgerald for once again opening the book covers for me. Karen Jones, you lit up the journey again and shared my unending enthusiasm and energy. To our designer Maria Fernandez and cover artist Linda Kosarin, this book flies and is a joy to read thanks to you. Also, Leigh Grossman and Joe Rhatigan.

To SIRIUS XM Radio—Mel Karmazin, Scott Greenstein, Steve Blatter, John Zellner, Kid Kelly and Gregg Steele for the amazing stage you gave me to continue my life's journey. A special thank you to Steve Leeds for his never-ending interest in archiving our history and his help in making this book so successful.

To Brian DeNicola, Annie Witten, and Alex DiTrolio for your constant research and information-gathering skills.

To my friends Laura and Bob Sillerman who shared an amazing new adventure with me; Joe McCoy who is always there and is the best resource in the business; Maria and Chris Angelo—you are and will always be part of this story; Terry Stewart and the Rock & Roll Hall of Fame and Museum—collecting our dreams and proving them to be true.

Once again to Ennio & Michael's Ristorante in Greenwich Village for providing our writing hideaway and great food. Also to Lure Restaurant in SoHo, where our creativity was enhanced by those writing lunches and to Robert Collins for his enthusiasm and those great deviled eggs.

I want to extend a very special thanks to Brian Wilson, who wrote our Foreword, Petula Clark, who wrote our Preface, and especially to Billy Joel, one of my favorite audience members—Wow! You are part of this amazing journey which continues today.

A special acknowledgment to my friend Roger Lefkon for his foresight and for never changing direction.

To Bobby, Elvis, Roy, Chuck, Neil, Jerry Lee, Frankie V, Frankie A, Brian and Petula, Johnny, Tommy J, Antoine, Shirley, Paul A, Mary and all 20,000 others who made this time travel possible—this is your history book.

Especially to my best friend, my wife Jodie for her absolute encouragement and loving participation. Thank you my darling, and thank you all!

...And The Beat Goes On!

Rich Maloof Thanks...

Cousin Brucie, who is not only eminently quotable but an unending source of good company. Thanks, Cuz, for sharing more than a decade of rock & roll memories and for your confidence that our collaboration would translate well onto the written page. And thanks to your lovely wife, Jodie, for her keen insights and killer chocolate cupcakes.

Thank you to f-Stop Fitzgerald of BAND-F, Ltd., for inviting me into the fold a second time around and always having an encouraging word.

Karen Jones shepherded this book to completion and enabled everyone to hit the deadline without ever wielding an iron fist. Thanks to copyeditor Leigh Grossman, designer Maria Fernandez and cover artist Linda Kosarin, to assistant editor Mie Kingsley, and contributor Troy Shaheen.

Thank you to Charlie Nurnberg, president and publisher of Imagine Publishing, for prodding but not prying. His faith in this project made it a possibility.

Christine M. Corso tirelessly transcribed hours upon hours of interviews. Thanks to Debra DeSalvo, my secret weapon, who is herself destined to make rock & roll history. Thanks also to Lenny DeGraf at the Thomas Edison Museum in West Orange, NJ.

This book's manuscript came together over several great meals in downtown New York City. Mille grazie once again to the hosts and wait staff at Ennio and Michael's Ristorante in Greenwich Village; to Robert & Co. at Lure Restaurant in SOHO; and to the good people at Chinatown Brasserie.

Thanks to HP Newquist, Pete Prown, and Lee Knife for loud riffs and louder laughs. To Mark Inglis for believing I'm a better writer than I understand myself to be. I wish I could name here all of the cousins, bandmates, and lifelong friends who forever keep me in high spirits and good music.

My parents, Mitchell and Teresa Maloof, introduced me to the Beatles, bought my first guitar, took me to my first concert (Neil Diamond!), and let me go see Kiss when I was twelve years old. How does anyone say thanks for all of that?

Finally, a standing ovation for the home team. Like everything I do, this book is for my cherie amour, Kris Aswad, and for our children Daniel, Tess, and James—the next generation of rock & roll.

PHOTO CREDITS

We want to thank Dave Booth of Showtime Archives in Canada for his dedication and cooperation in providing the terrific images in this book. Thanks to Weston Minissali of Preferable Tapioca, LLC for the digital scans. With the exception of the photography credits below, all images were acquired from Showtime Archives.

Images from Photofest (photofestnyc.com)
Pgs. 20, 67, 68, 77, 78, 87, 90, 91, 92, 95, 110, 120, 126, 127, 128, 136, 141, 145, 148, 152, 153, 154, 155, 165, 168, 169, 170, 183, 184, 190, 191, 192, 193, 204, 205, 206, 212, 213, 217, 220, 235, 236, 240, 260, 266, 267, 268, 286, 292, 293, 294, 295, 298

Images from BigStockPhoto.com
Pgs. 1, 19, 31, 57, 97, 159, 209, 245, 279, endpapers: 45 vinyl record, © Murat Baysan, Big Stock Photo.com
Pgs. 2-3: © Aleksandar Bracinac, Big Stock Photo.com
Pgs. 6-7: © Wolfgang Amri, Big Stock Photo.com
Pgs. 8-9, 248-249, 310-311, 312-313: background art © Sophie Bengtsson, Big Stock Photo.com
Pgs. 18, 306: © Fulya Bayraktaroglu, Big Stock Photo.com
Pg. 23: © David Martyn, Big Stock Photo.com
Pg. 55: plaque, © Danny Hooks, Big Stock Photo.com
Pg. 180: © Lucia Corona, Big Stock Photo.com
Pgs. 212-213: peace sign, © Georgios Kollidas, Big Stock Photo.com
Pg. 225: © Mario Ragma, Big Stock Photo.com
Pg. 229: © Wayne Kelly, Big Stock Photo.com
Pg. 254: © Andres Rodriguez, Big Stock Photo.com
Pg. 269: © Emilian Mihailescu, Big Stock Photo.com
Pgs. 314, endpapers: piano keys detail, © Mikko Pitkänen, Big Stock Photo.com
Endpapers: base guitar detail © Brittany Bastian, Big Stock Photo.com; drum set © Vladimir Mucibabic, Big Stock Photo.com; retro microphone © Slavoljub Pantelic, Big Stock Photo.com; saxophone © Vladislav Lebedinski, Big Stock Photo.com; keyboards © Nicole Marquardt, Big Stock Photo.com; vintage bass © P. J, Big Stock Photo.com; detail of drum © Fernando Carniel Machado, Big Stock Photo.com; microphone © Angelo Gilardelli, Big Stock Photo.com

Images from Bruce Morrow
Pgs. 16, 24, 28

Images from f-stop Fitzgerald
Background art: 10-11, 12-13, 14-15, 16-17; Pg. 111: Batman images; Album Covers: 98, 106, 122, 134, 138, 139, 160, 172, 178, 210, 218, 252, 262, 300, 302

Other Image Sources
Pg. 9: Brian Wilson © James Minchin III
Pg. 11: Petula Clark, © Harry Langdon
Pg. 13: Courtesy of the Steve Blauner/Bobby Darin Testamentary Trust
Pg. 115: Courtesy of Donald Farr, Mustang Monthly magazine
Pg. 307: Karen Jones
Pg. 314: Billy Joel, © Greg Gorman